DREISERANA

DREISERANA
A BOOK ABOUT HIS BOOKS

BY

VREST ORTON

HASKELL HOUSE PUBLISHERS LTD.
Publishers of Scarce Scholarly Books
NEW YORK, N. Y. 10012
1973

HASKELL HOUSE PUBLISHERS Ltd.
Publishers of Scarce Scholarly Books
280 LAFAYETTE STREET
NEW YORK, N. Y. 10012

Library of Congress Cataloging in Publication Data

Orton, Vrest, 1897–
    Dreiserana; a book about his books.

    A list of errata and addenda to E. D. McDonald's
A bibliography of the writings of Theodore Dreiser,
1928.
    Original ed. issued in series: The Chocorua
bibliographies.
    1. Dreiser, Theodore, 1871–1945--Bibliography.
I. McDonald, Edward David. A bibliography of the
writings of Theodore Dreiser. II. Title.
Z8241.7.O77 1973   016.813'5'2   72–6287
ISBN 0–8383–1629–8

Printed in the United States of America

FOR
ALICE & MELVIN TEACHOUT

A CHECK-LIST AND INDEX

A CHECK-LIST AND INDEX

PART II

PART III

PART IV

DREISERANA

PROLEGOMENA

The task of bringing this work through four years to something approaching completion has left the writer impressed with one thing; there must be a Dreiser hoodoo. Close attention paid to the history of Dreiser's books and to the vicissitudes attending their publications, mutations and suppressions will indeed reveal it. It seems, further, that comparable untowardness has followed every person who ever deigned to touch a finger to the business of compiling Dreiser bibliographies. They have either disappeared from the scene, lost interest in first editions or allowed their contemplated books to remain unwritten, incomplete, or unpublished.

The veteran of Dreiser enthusiasts and the first person, so far as is known, to become interested in studying and listing the bibliographic points in Dreiser's books was Mr. W. W. Lange, of Milwaukee, Wisconsin. Mr. Lange is a personal friend of Dreiser and has kept up a correspondence with him since they first became acquainted in 1920. During this time Mr. Lange wrote critical appreciations of Dreiser, collected first editions and MSS. and went into the bibliographic history of Dreiser's writings. He contemplated, at one time, writing a formal bibliography, but being a very busy man could only approach work of that kind as an avocation. The bibliography never took definite shape beyond a check-list contributed to *The Publisher's Weekly*.

But Mr. Lange kept up correspondence with other Dreiser collectors over a period of ten years, and in several instances, freely placed invaluable information of one kind or another at the disposal of bibliographers, especially this writer. To Mr. Lange must go much credit for beginning and enhancing the Dreiser first-edition interest now so widespread and salubrious. Every collector and every bibliographer of Dreiser is deeply indebted to him. The gratitude of the writer of this book can not be over-emphasized. In 1929, Mr. Lange apparently lost interest in first editions and disposed of his library.

In 1922, Mr. George Rodier Hyde, then a writer for the *Los Angeles Examiner*, became a Dreiser collector and did considerable research. He began to assemble a bibliography which was to be privately printed and circulated, but it came to nothing . . . at least, it was never printed.

In 1921, a person in New York City, whose name I shall not mention, began to suggest, in a series of carefully worded letters to Dreiser, that he be appointed official Dreiser bibliographer. Dreiser, over a period extending from May 13, 1921, to March 22, 1922, wrote him a number of letters of considerable length about the proposed bibliography. Dreiser placed at this "bibliographer's" disposal a wealth of important and exclusive information. Dreiser's early letters evidence an almost naïve feeling of confidence in the other man. Then they range down to the dawning of the truth, when it was evident in Dreiser's own words to him: "Most people have been content to obtain one signature, but you have appeared to me, at times, to be doing rather a Dreiser signature business. . . . If that has anything to do with the preparation or non-preparation of this bibliography, I will be very glad to dispense with the bibliography." Dreiser wrote later to a friend regarding this opportunist: "He pestered me for three years for autographs, and finally, as a bait to interest me, planned a fanciful bibliography, which was to sell for $7.50. But when he found that I would not sign the packages of books he began sending me, he dropped that." In the end, after accomplishing his purpose of eliciting a large sheaf of Dreiser letters, this "bibliographer" stopped writing Dreiser, turned about and sold Dreiser's entire series of letters for a high price. He also sold the set of first editions that he had got Dreiser to sign—obtaining prices considerably above those of unsigned copies, as may well be imagined. This enterprising person continued in business in New York for some years afterwards, but finally left for other hunting grounds.

In 1923, a firm of booksellers in Philadelphia announced that Mr. H. L. R. Swire, the author of a bibliography of Joseph Hergesheimer, was to write, and they to publish, a bibliography of Theodore Dreiser. Nothing further was ever heard of that.

No bibliography of Dreiser was actually announced in the years 1924 and 1925, but in 1926 this writer began, at the request of a firm of booksellers in Philadelphia, to prepare a definitive work on

Dreiser. He got Dreiser to write an introduction for it and it was announced in an advertisement. In a letter from this firm appeared the sentence: "The unfortunate bibliographer can not count upon receiving anything more material than the satisfaction derived from accomplishing a congenial task." It must have been missed entirely by the writer of this book, for not until he came to deliver his manuscript, and that of Dreiser, was he apprised of its real meaning. Consequently, the manuscript was never delivered. He returned Dreiser's manuscript, by request, to Dreiser.

In 1927, the same booksellers announced that a bibliography of Dreiser was in preparation by Prof. Edward D. McDonald, an able writer and author of bibliographies of D. H. Lawrence, and Norman Douglas. It was to be published in 1928, with so many signed copies. In 1928 it was published. There were no signed copies, for Dreiser would not sign any. The book was not definitive . . . its sins, however, were largely of omission.

This writer then determined to publish, at once, a list of errata and addenda, so that collectors might, with both, have a more definitive and correct check of Dreiser's books. He took from his original book-manuscript all the material that was not in McDonald's book, corrected the latter, and made an article which he "sold" to *The American Collector*, a monthly magazine edited by a New York bookseller. Soon after the article was accepted (but not paid for) the bookseller went into bankruptcy, and the magazine died, never again to be published.

This bookseller, however, printed, without the author's permission, 150 copies of the article, in the form of a pamphlet entitled "Notes to Add to a Bibliography of Theodore Dreiser" which he evidently sold. He then left New York, and has not been heard of since.

So ends, up to this year of grace, the history, so far as known to this author of what he chooses to term the Dreiser hoodoo. The way of the bibliographer is hard and thankless, but apparently that of the Dreiser bibliographer is fatal. No pity, however, should be lavished upon any one except Dreiser himself. One can only imagine the state of his temper after ten years of continual requests to furnish bibliographic data to one after another of his bibliographers; ten years of watching while each of these ventures has come to grief. It is small wonder that Mr. Dreiser is not exactly enthusiastic over the pastime of collecting his first editions.

Very frankly, this writer would prefer this book to evidence his profound relief at having finished with Dreiser bibliographies for all time, than to suggest any smirk of self-satisfaction.

It may be well to emphasize here just what the reader should expect from this book. He should *not* expect a complete bibliography of the writings of Theodore Dreiser. Prof. McDonald published in his book a wealth of bibliographical data with collations of the first editions in full, which there is no need to duplicate here. There were, however, certain "points" left out of Prof. McDonald's book (through no fault of his), and also facts necessary to a clearer and more complete understanding of the publications of Theodore Dreiser. The writer's intention is to print this material here, together with a certain amount of errata to the McDonald volume as well as certain new material which will bring up to date the history and listing of Dreiser's writings since the McDonald book was published.

When NOTES TO ADD TO A BIBLIOGRAPHY OF THEODORE DREISER was prepared, in some haste, for the magazine publication (and printed unknown to this writer, as a pamphlet) there was no intention to slight, depreciate, or lay open to criticism Prof. McDonald's work. Rather, the hope was to supply what material the writer then had in his possession, so that, used in connection with McDonald's book, it might round out a more complete bibliography. Unfortunately, the result fell far short of the intention. The impression got about that the pamphlet was a direct criticism done in a spirit which could only be interpreted as unkind. Nothing could be further from the truth. The writer hopes that this book, in which he has made every attempt to emphasize the importance of Prof. McDonald's work, and its absolute necessity to the collector, will, in part, make up for the unintentional injury that may have been done to Prof. McDonald.

During the last four years a host of persons have been extremely kind and have put themselves out in many ways to aid this writer. It is a pleasure to acknowledge here his gratitude and thanks for the help and encouragement of:—

Mr. Ralph Allan	Mr. Raymond Bond
Mr. Rexford Barton	Mr. William Briggs
Mr. Ashley Belbin	Miss Emily Cecelin

Mr. Bennett Cerf
Mr. Walter Coates
Captain Louis H. Cohn
Miss L. A. Comstock
Mr. W. Paul Cook
Mr. R. P. Conway
Miss Isabel Devoy
Mr. Jas. H. Drake
Mr. Theodore Dreiser
Mr. Burton Emmett
Mr. Louis Feipel
Mr. Donald Friede
Miss Mary Gold
Mr. Alfred Goldsmith
Mr. Ward Greene
Mr. Albert H. Gross
Mr. Irving Halpern
Mr. Morton Hiscox
Mr. E. J. Hirle
Mr. Joseph Harper
Mr. Paul Johnston

Mr. J. Jefferson Jones
Mr. W. W. Lange
Mr. Henry Lanier
Mr. William C. Lengel
Miss Amy Loveman
Mr. James Mac Namee
Mr. H. L. Mencken
Mr. Julian Messner
Mr. David Moss
Mrs. Rose L. Orton
Mr. Eugene Reynal
Mr. Freemont Rider
Mr. Arthur Rushmore
Mr. Frank Shay
Mr. Thomas Smith
Mr. H. D. Sohns
Mr. R. T. Stites
Mr. Gilbert Troxell
Mr. B. W. Willett
Mr. John T. Winterich
Mr. Merton Yewdale

PART I

THE DREISER BOOKS

[1] "STUDIES OF CONTEMPORARY CELEBRITIES"

In the McDonald bibliography there are, approximately, three pages of the *Introduction* devoted to a discussion of this mythical volume . . . a discussion that arrives nowhere except at an assumption that such a book may exist or, on the other hand, may not. There is in sight, as a matter of fact, much available evidence pointing to its existence. It was listed by Dreiser when he was asked to write a biographical note for WHO'S WHO IN AMERICA, and it appeared as the title of a published volume in the 1899-1900 edition of that compilation of American "celebrities." It was listed in every subsequent edition up to that of 1903-1905, in which it was put down as out-of-print. In A DICTIONARY OF AMERICAN AUTHORS (1901), this title also appeared as a publication of Mr. Dreiser. STUDIES OF CONTEMPORARY CELEBRITIES was mentioned in the *Notes and Queries* department of *The American Mercury*, where a bookseller claimed to have seen a man who had viewed a copy. Several American writers, one recalls, referred to it as Dreiser's first and "rarest" book, stating that the collector who picked up a copy would be lucky. Indeed, such a legend grew up over a period of thirty years, that one began to believe in the book's actuality. Certainly a horde of collectors were always on the lookout for it, and dealers advertised and sent "scouts" widespread in the quest. Yet no copy of STUDIES OF CONTEMPORARY CELEBRITIES came to light . . . which was natural, for no such book was ever printed or published.

The evidence is contained in a letter that Dreiser wrote November 10, 1921, in answer to an inquiry about the famous "book."

The excerpt from that letter, which follows, was placed at my disposal by Mr. W. W. Lange, who had it in his possession. It is included here with Mr. Dreiser's permission.

"As for STUDIES OF CONTEMPORARY CELEBRITIES," Dreiser wrote, "that was a manuscript which I prepared for a Cincinnati publishing house whose name, at the moment, escapes me, but whose agent in New York caused me to prepare the same on a promise of $500 on delivery of the MS. It was to have been sold on subscription, I think. The MS was prepared, but before the check came, the concern went into the hands of a receiver, and I got no check, and had a hard time getting the MS. I was a mere kid and a little anxious to see a book of mine in print. Hence, in 1899, I stuck an announcement of it in WHO'S WHO because I had a call for data about myself. Later I threw the thing in a trunk, along with the other early things, and now I do not know where the trunk is. But the same contains a LIFE OF GEORGE INNES, prepared for another New York concern, which is a good thing which I wish I had. Mrs. Innes, as well as his son-in-law, Scott Hartley, the sculptor, helped me to prepare it. There are also early poems, and all sorts of unpublished articles which sometime may turn up to plague me. If I knew where it was, I would have it sent on here, and would do some burning."

This, it seems to me, is one of the most illuminating pieces that Dreiser ever wrote. It definitely settles the controversy for all time . . . but it does more than that. It points out the existence of the manuscript of an entirely unknown work, THE LIFE OF GEORGE INNES, and of many other unpublished pieces, which may turn up some day. SISTER CARRIE and one or two other Dreiser items are difficult to come by nowadays, but if the book-hunter wants a real quest to set himself upon, let him lay plans to discover this trunk.

[2] A PRINCESS OF ARCADY
by Arthur Henry. *New York, 1900.*

To anyone who has closely scanned the preliminary pages of the first edition of SISTER CARRIE, the name of Arthur Henry will seem familiar, for that book was dedicated to him. Mr. Henry, so I am told, is alive, but my efforts to locate him have failed. I shall have to be content to insert here the transcript of an interview which Dreiser gave me sometime during February, 1927, in response to my request for the story of his planning and writing of SISTER CARRIE. Here also appears the story of the book listed above by Arthur Henry, and one that I put down as belonging to a set of Dreiser books. It might be interesting to scan other books by Arthur Henry of which there were three or four during the period of his association with Dreiser. What follows here is not direct quotation, but what I was able directly after the interview to make out from notes taken of Dreiser's conversation.

When Mr. Dreiser first began to write, during the last part of the 19th century, he formed a friendship with Arthur Henry, who, already an author, was attempting to make his living by the pen. Dreiser insinuated that for a long time it was a hard pull. Henry was following the usual and easiest road to success for a hack-writer by doing articles on all kinds of subjects. Dreiser naturally falling under his influence, and looking to him as a man who had already achieved the glamorous distinction of appearing in print, began to write articles himself. From 1897, when Dreiser's first piece appeared in any magazine, to 1900, all his published contributions, with the exception of a few poems, were articles. He and Henry worked together a great deal on the pieces they were both publishing . . . it was sometimes difficult to tell which of the two was the author of some of the articles. Dreiser, with Henry's encouragement and help had perfected his own technique, so that he was pretty sure of selling anything he wanted to write, but strangely enough, he never thought of tackling a short story. It was Henry who first suggested the notion to him, and it was Henry who got Dreiser (while Dreiser was making a visit in Toledo, Ohio) to write his first short story. At the same time Henry had begun a short story of his own, and they worked together on the two, both of which they sold. After this, they collaborated on other short stories, many of which were successful.

It was about this time that Henry began to write a novel. It was evidently his virgin effort in this medium. Many times during its construction, he became discouraged and was about to drop it. Dreiser then encouraged Henry to go on with the work and finally all was done except the last chapter. Henry was stuck. He would not, or could not finish the thing. Dreiser, bound that it should be completed, wrote the last chapter himself. The book was A PRINCESS OF ARCADY. It was published by Doubleday, Page, N. Y., 1900. I have no doubt that it ought to belong in a collected set of Dreiserana as a very rare item.

After this, Henry convinced Dreiser that his forte lay in writing longer things than articles and short stories, and that he ought to start a novel. This was good advice, for it produced SISTER CARRIE, which Dreiser began to write in the autumn of 1899. After a long travail during which time Dreiser in turn often wanted to give up and chuck the manuscript into the wastebasket, the book was finished in May, 1900, solely through Henry's encouragement and almost forceful urging. It does not take a magician to see that Dreiser owes a great deal to Arthur Henry, which debt he sought to repay by the dedication to SISTER CARRIE, which reads as follows: "To My Friend, Arthur Henry, whose steadfast ideals, and serene devotion to truth and beauty have served to lighten the method and strengthen the purpose of this volume."

The manuscript of SISTER CARRIE was first submitted to Harper

& Bros. Dreiser took it to Henry Mills Alden, editor of *Harper's Magazine*, whose advice regarding the acceptance of book manuscripts was held in high esteem by the publishing house. Alden read the manuscript and told Dreiser that it was an able piece of work, and that it ought to be published, but doubted very much if any publisher would accept it. No one knew better than Alden the state of the American mind of that age. It was in the mass, highly suspicious of free expression of any kind, and in 1900 the book Dreiser called SISTER CARRIE was somewhat freer than any American novel Mr. Alden or anyone else had set their eyes upon. Nevertheless, Alden turned it over to the publishing branch of Harpers with his recommendation, and about three weeks later Harpers informed Dreiser that they could not publish it. Alden then reiterated his admiration for the book, and suggested to Dreiser that he take it to Doubleday, Page, which company he thought might be in a better position to consider it.

In the meantime, Frank Norris, having gained considerable renown by the publication of McTEAGUE, had been installed as reader for Doubleday, Page. (It is interesting to note that thirty years later Dreiser wrote an introduction to McTEAGUE, in the first collected edition of Frank Norris.) Norris devoted half his time to reading for the firm, and the other half to writing. When Dreiser carried the manuscript of SISTER CARRIE to this firm, Norris was the first to see it and was at once carried away with enthusiasm for the book. He conveyed this feeling to other members of the company, Frank Doubleday, Walter Hines Page, S. A. Everitt, and Henry W. Lanier, all of whom read it with no less feeling of its importance. They concluded that Doubleday, Page ought to publish SISTER CARRIE. Page wrote Dreiser a letter of congratulation. Dreiser, after leaving the manuscript with Norris, went off to Missouri. Morgan Robertson, whom Dreiser had come to know, and who had in fact been the first person to tell Dreiser about Frank Norris, learned during Dreiser's absence that Doubleday, Page had accepted the book. He went to Arthur Henry with the news, and it was in a letter from Henry that Dreiser first learned that his book was to be brought out. He came back to New York to sign a contract with the publishers. The book was then printed.

Dreiser went on to tell how in the meantime, Mrs. Frank Doubleday read the book, and was horrified by its frankness. Mrs. Doubleday was an ardent social worker and active in movements of a highly moral order. She not only determined SISTER CARRIE was no book for the firm of Doubleday, Page to publish, but actually took a violent dislike to it, and everything connected with it. This feeling lasted for years, and was never mitigated. It resulted in the firm retracting its decision to go on with SISTER CARRIE.

Dreiser had again left New York and it was during his absence that he received a letter from Frank Norris saying that Doubleday, Page had decided not to continue with the book. Dreiser returned to New York for a talk with Norris, who still wanted SISTER CARRIE to come before the American public, feeling that this was the only way to substantiate his own admiration. He therefore advised Dreiser to insist that the company carry out its contract to the fullest extent. This Dreiser did.

The legal adviser to the firm of Doubleday, Page was called in (as he told Dreiser later) and he advised that the firm was obliged to go on and publish the book. But publishing a book did not necessarily entail selling it. It might be printed and bound, but also the copies of it might conceivably be thrown into the cellar. This advice was evidently taken, in the opinion of Mr. Dreiser. Certainly, Mr. Dreiser says, no copies were ever sold. But Frank Norris managed to send out some copies to the reviewers. Dreiser thinks that there must have been about a hundred copies distributed this way.

The news that Dreiser had written a dirty book was talked about on all sides. He had become, in 1900, a fairly successful author in a financial sense, and was making about $4,000 a year, a large sum in those days. Most magazines were ready to buy his stuff. But upon the news of the SISTER CARRIE debacle, the bottom dropped out of his success, and magazines began to refuse everything from his pen. He found himself up against the necessity of making a living in some other way. Even when he looked for a job outside the literary world, he found the ever-increasing opposition to him that SISTER CARRIE and its "suppression" had generated in the minds of the public. Discouraged, he went to Virginia where he stopped for a while and began to write JENNIE GERHARDT. When a few chapters were done, he brought it back to New York, hoping to get some publisher to take this book. He first went to John Phillips of the publishing house of Phillips and McClure, but Phillips would have nothing to do with JENNIE GERHARDT or any other Dreiser book. Phillips cited as evidence of the feeling against Dreiser, the story of a woman in Boston who had become so incensed at the book, SISTER CARRIE, that she tore it up and threw it into the fireplace. [Here is one hint, at least, to prove that SISTER CARRIE got beyond the reviewers.] Dreiser then took the manuscript of JENNIE GERHARDT to A. S. Barnes, who also refused to publish it.

Deciding that no headway could be made until the SISTER CARRIE affair blew over, Dreiser gave up writing and went through a period of job hunting, which is touched upon in THE "GENIUS," where he writes of actually working in a section gang for a New York railroad. After this he sought an editorial job and went to work for Street and Smith. Here he edited one of their magazines, and also many paper bound novels.

[3] SISTER CARRIE.
New York, 1900.

Whereas, in the case of STUDIES OF CONTEMPORARY CELEBRITIES, there was a legend about a book which never existed in print, there is a more often-discussed legend about SISTER CARRIE, a book everyone knows does exist, although in comparatively small numbers. Apart from the many first edition dealers and experts who have guessed at the truth of the legend, such well known writers as H. L. Mencken, Burton Rascoe, and Frank Harris have also taken a look at it. They have, in the main, agreed that Doubleday, Page did print the book, but "suppressed" it before any but review copies got out, "throwing into the cellar" what remained of the edition. Mr. Dreiser, from the interview just printed above, apparently gives this same idea the mark of truth. McDonald seems to support much the same rumor, adding that Doubleday, Page certainly do not know how many copies were printed or sent out. After guessing that 100 would cover the number of copies in existence, he disdains to follow further the "highly conjectural piece of business."

It seemed to me from the beginning that Doubleday, Page should know, if they could be got to search their records, the number of copies printed, sold, given away or "burnt" of SISTER CARRIE. For several years attempts were made to secure this information. In reply to one letter, Mr. S. A. Everitt, of the firm of Doubleday, Page wrote as follows:

"We have a record of the publication date, November 8, 1900. There is no other available record here, and my recollection is that Doubleday, Page and Company printed a first edition of 1000 to 2000 copies of the book which was sold *in the regular way* to the trade, and copies sent out to the newspapers for review, and the distribution of the book carried on in the regular way, the same as any other novel published at the time, until Harper & Brothers bought the plates and rights . . . I think at the suggestion of the author."

While Mr. Everitt's letter is based wholly on his opinion and memory, it gives some indication of the truth. To know that *any* copies had been *sold in the regular way to the trade* was to know considerably more than any one had known before. It was an appetizer to seek further and obtain the facts from actual records. I determined to obtain a statement from Mr. Frank Doubleday. In reply to a letter asking for a transcript of the records, the following letter was received from Mr. Doubleday's secretary:

"I am not at all sure that the analysis and sales records going back to the year 1900 are available, and so far we have resisted going through the accumulation of twenty-eight years in our store room to try to get at the definite facts in regard to Sister Carrie. However, if you will give us a few days, we will make the search and see what we can find.
"In the recollection of those of us who were here at the time, no copies of the book were destroyed, burned, remaindered, or otherwise disposed of than by sale, or sending out as review copies, but we will write you further in a few days, if we are able to find any definite details."

Again, here was more data to send the investigation a bit nearer its end. It is interesting to note that in the recollection of those concerned, no copies were remaindered. A day or so later, another letter was received from Mr. Doubleday's secretary, which contained the whole story in a nutshell. It read:

"These are the actual facts about Sister Carrie, as revealed by the analysis card.
"The first edition consisted of 1,008 copies, of which 129 were sent out for review, 465 were sold, and the balance, 423 copies, were turned over. to J. F. Taylor & Company."

Here, for the first time, was the exact history of this much-discussed first edition. The firm of J. F. Taylor & Company was a remainder house very active in the book business about 1900. They made a practice of buying remainders and trade books from publishers, and selling them by subscription, which meant selling them by post, or by house-to-house canvass. They are no longer in business. We can only assume that the 423 copies of SISTER CARRIE that Doubleday sold them, were sold by them, in turn, to 423 housewives, who unless they read it probably used the volume for divers purposes . . . an ornament for the parlor (it has a pretty red cover) or something for the baby to play with. As to the scarcity of SISTER CARRIE . . . it is much scarcer than is generally supposed. Before any data were known as to the number of copies printed, McDonald and others guessed that it was not so scarce as made out. On the contrary, a book printed in 1900 to the number of only 1008 copies, nearly half of them remaindered (everyone knows the fate of remainders) leaving only 546 actually sold to the trade, is, in 1930, a very scarce book. In the course of thirty years, any edition of 1000 copies of a novel will, for the most part, become lost, destroyed, or worn out. And most of the copies that do exist, will not do so in a very good state. SISTER CARRIE was cheaply bound and cheaply stamped, so most copies one sees nowadays are in only "fair" condition.

I once had the opportunity to see a copy of the first edition of SISTER CARRIE in very good condition, with one exception. The last page of printing (page 557) had been literally torn in two, and the lower half lost. The book, of course, was worth little. Some months later, I saw another copy of what was offered as a first edition of SISTER CARRIE. It had the right binding, lettering, title-page and every point in the collation checked up . . . with one exception. The lining papers were not of the same laid-antique paper as the body of the book. This aroused suspicion, and upon minute examination the following discovery was made. The book had been made up with the case and title-page of the 1900 SISTER CARRIE, but the body of the thing was that of the second edition issued by Dodge in 1907. It had been a simple matter (because the 1907 edition was printed from the same plates) to insert the body of that edition, consisting of pages 1 to 557 into the binding of the 1900 edition with a little care in leaving in the preliminary pages, numbers i to viii. One should examine carefully any SISTER CARRIE with special attention to the fact that the real first must have in front, one leaf blank on both sides, and in back two leaves all blank. And, moreover, all pages, including lining papers, must be laid-antique paper, not wove.

In the two stories that belong to the highly interesting legend of the "suppression" of the first edition by its publishers and the "burning in the cellar" of the remainder, one sees in them, on the authority of the facts from the Doubleday analysis card, nothing but hearsay and rumor. Mr. Frank Doubleday has finally gone on record here that so many copies were printed, so many sold to the trade, so many given to reviewers, and so many remaindered to the Taylor house. This leaves not a single loop-hole for any copies to have been "cast into the furnace" or "thrown into the cellar for employees to help themselves to," as the stories run. Anyone, of course, may interpret these facts as he pleases, but no one can fail, I think, to interpret the conditions surrounding the publication of Dreiser's first book as decidedly unfavorable to Dreiser. To him, it could have seemed nothing but a fiasco. It can easily be assumed, without too much imagination, that Doubleday, Page did not burn up much energy in getting SISTER CARRIE into the bookshops. That only 465 were sold to dealers, must point to a peculiar lethargy on the part of the many Doubleday book drummers, or else to some kind of influence toward limitation of sales. Or else (and both sides should have their say) the book would not sell, and so died a natural death and was buried, as all unsuccessful books are, in a remainder house.

After it was all over, the plates from which the book had been printed were turned back to Dreiser with, as I was told, a cheque for $500.00. He kept the plates until 1907, when the B. W. Dodge Company used them for the second time. It is interesting to note that these same plates were used, from first to last, by six different publishers, to print six different issues of the book.

[4] SISTER CARRIE
(The first English edition *London*, 1901)

In a good many ways, the first English SISTER CARRIE published by Heinemann, is the most interesting, and perhaps the scarcest (except the first American) of all Dreiser books. Further, it is of more than commercial value to the collector. Published in 1901, six

SISTER CARRIE

BY

THEODORE DREISER

LONDON: WILLIAM HEINEMANN. 1901

years before it was really brought to the attention of the public at large in the United States, the Heinemann edition reached the English public to the number of 1500 copies the first year. It unquestionably won for Dreiser his first praise and favorable renown as a novelist. The first edition was for 1500 copies. The same year 1000 more sets of sheets were printed, but only 250 sets were bound up. The remaining 750 copies were held until 1910, when they were bound in paper wrappers, and jobbed to W. H. Smith & Sons. In 1912, the 250 copies of the second printing above referred to, were sold to Grant Richards, the English publisher. There was a copy of the 1910 paper-bound issue (which is really only a third English issue and practically worthless) offered, in a pretty slip case, by a New York bookseller for $35.00 . . . a hint that all booksellers' catalogues should not be taken verbatim.

The first Heinemann edition, however, is decidedly scarce . . . in my experience, next to the first American in that respect. I have never seen a copy in fine state. The cover was stamped in white ink, which easily wears off, and further, after three years of advertising in England for a copy, I have not been able to find one. Strangely enough, the book is in one respect, unique, since it is against the laws of the United States to possess a copy . . . or even to import one. The book was brought out in the Heinemann Dollar Library, and had on one of the preliminary pages a half-tone illustration of an American one dollar bill.

In addition to all this, the English first is, in no wise, the same book that Doubleday, Page brought out in America in 1901, or that other American publishers subsequently issued from the American plates. It was a revised and re-written book, being 200 pages shorter than the American editions. It is more important to consider the Heinemann edition as the first revised edition than as the first English edition of an American book. Rumor has it that Frank Norris did the expurgating, both parts of that sentence being untrue; the book was not expurgated and Norris had no hand in its revision. It was cut down by Arthur Henry, Dreiser's friend, and by Dreiser himself. Norris took part only in influencing Heinemann to bring out the book in England. It might be well to explain here that, in no sense, was the book cut to remove objectionable features raised in the so-called suppression that was supposed to have occurred in America. It was cut by Mr. Heinemann's request, so it would conform in size to the other volumes in the Dollar Library. Dreiser comments upon this point in a letter written March 22, 1922:

> "The English edition of SISTER CARRIE was cut by me at the request of Mr. Heinemann, who would not publish the book unless it was so cut. And since it had been suppressed here, I thought it best to bring it out there regardless, even though I had to cut it. It has since been published in the American form in England. It was cut in 1901, the spring, I think, and published in England the same year."

Mr. W. W. Lange, whose opinion must be listened to with respect when Dreiser is concerned, says, "Knowing Dreiser's attitude as well as I do, I know he would not cut anything out that he thought should stay in a book, whether it was suppressed or not." To which one must emphatically agree.

The "American form" that Dreiser refers to in his letter above is the Harper edition published in London in May, 1912. Constable, another London publisher, also published an edition in May, 1927.

The collation of the first Heinemann English edition is as follows:

SISTER CARRIE

Published July 31, 1901.

TITLE PAGE

Sister Carrie / (a double rule) / By Theodore Dreiser / (Publisher's device) / (a double rule) / London: William Heinemann. 1901 (Whole enclosed in double rule box).

PAGES

Pp. viii plus 1-(360). Consisting of (i): The Dollar Library / of American Fiction / (a page of text). (verso): The Dollar Library / (a page of text) / London: William Heinemann. (iii): (facsimile of a dollar bill) / The following Volumes are now ready:- / (lists seven titles). Beside the last title, the word "September." / Other Volumes in preparation. / The Dollar Library. / A Monthly Series of American Fiction. / London: William Heinemann. / And at all Booksellers and Bookstalls. (verso): Blank. (v): The Dollar Library / (a rule) / Sister Carrie (verso): The Dollar Library / of American Fiction / (a rule) / The Girl at the Halfway House. / by E. Hough. / Parlous Times. / by David Dwight Wells. / Lords of the North. / by Agnes C. Laut. / The Chronic Loafer. / by Nelson Lloyd. / Her Mountain Lover. / by Hamlin Garland. / Sister Carrie. / by Theodore Dreiser. / The Darlingtons. / by E. Peake. / (a rule) / London: Wm. Heinemann. / (the whole enclosed with single rule box). (vii): (Title page as above). (verso): (at lower left

hand corner): This edition enjoys copyright in / all countries signatory to
the Berne / Treaty, and is not to be imported into / the United States of
America / Text: 1-357. Pages 358 to 360 unnumbered. Page 358: Printed
by / Morrison and Gibb, Limited / Edinburgh

BINDING

7 1/4 by 4 7/8. Issued in green, woven cloth, stamped in white and
black inks. All edges cut, top gilded.
FRONT COVER: The Dollar Library / (a design of circle 2 1/2 inches
in diameter, composed of eagle on American flag with the Capitol Building
in background. Part of background stamped in white ink, part in slate
colored ink. Flag and eagle blind stamped with black outlining, circle
in black.) / Sister Carrie / (whole enclosed in double rule box, stamped in
black.)

BACKBONE

SISTER / CARRIE / (a dot) / Theodore / Dreiser / (all stamped in white)
(publisher's device, stamped in black) Heinemann (stamped in black). The
book is printed on antique laid paper, the lining papers are wove paper.
The last eight-page signature consisting of pages 353-(360) are printed
on wove paper.
Some copies of this book have thirty-two pages of publisher's adver-
tisements tipped into the back.

[5] SISTER CARRIE
(The Dodge Edition) *New York, 1907*

Sometime before 1907, three men got together and formed a
publishing company. They were Mr. B. W. Dodge, Mr. Rickey,
and Mr. Dreiser. Dreiser, evidently thought the time was ripe to
bring out SISTER CARRIE. Six years had passed since the Doubleday
edition and he probably believed, sensibly enough, that the repute
gained from the English critics, and from his magazine articles in
this country, would make for the popularity of a new edition of
SISTER CARRIE. And, as it happened, he was correct. The Dodge
edition of SISTER CARRIE sold extremely well. It went through
several different printings, and helped establish the B. W. Dodge
Company as up and coming publishers.

The bibliographer of Dreiser perhaps wishes that it had not gone
through so many printings, for Mr. Dodge chose to invest each
printing with a slight change in the binding, stamping, or preliminary pages, making a pretty mess to straighten out. Since this, the
second American and the first illustrated edition, is scarce enough to
warrant considerable consideration, I have spent much time and

23

effort to discover which of half a dozen or so issues was the first. The following variants of the Dodge edition have been examined.

> A: Red woven cloth binding, words SISTER CARRIE on front cover stamped in gold, and this inscription on the copyright page *Press of / Braunworth & Co. / Bookbinders and Printers / Brooklyn, N. Y.*
> B: Same binding, words SISTER CARRIE on front cover stamped in yellow ink, same inscription on copyright page.
> C: Same binding, same stamping as (B), no printer's name on copyright page.
> D: Same binding, SISTER CARRIE on cover in gold, no printer's name on copyright page.
> E: Bound in blue woven cloth, same stamping as (A), same inscription as (A).

All variants have the ornament of a broken dish on the front cover stamped in gold. The issues that McDonald collates as the first is, so far as I can make out, the one described above under (C), which is not the first. The first is described under (A). What happened was this: Dodge had the book printed up in so many sets of sheets. For the first issue, (A above) he took a certain number of sheets and bound them up in a red cloth case, stamping SISTER CARRIE on the cover in gold . . . in other words making the best looking book he could for the money. The printer's name was on the copyright page of this batch of sheets. The book began to sell and another lot was needed, so the remainder of the same sheets were taken, and this time put into a case costing a little less, owing to stamping SISTER CARRIE on the front cover in yellow ink instead of gold. Another printing was now required, but this time Dodge went to another printer, whose name does not appear on the copyright page in place of *Braunworth's*, which came off. These subsequently printed sets of sheets were used for all later issues, as described above in (C) and (D). The blue cloth cannot be accounted for except as a whim of the publisher to vary colors yet for some reason this is a much scarcer issue. Other colors may turn up from time to time.

In 1908, Grosset and Dunlap, the reprint publishers, brought out SISTER CARRIE, using the same plates. McDonald states, curiously enough, that their edition was "with a much richer investiture than that of Doubleday, Page and Company." This is hard to understand, for the Grosset edition was certainly on cheaper paper, being wove, instead of laid-antique; it was bound in a low-count, thin, cheap cloth; and with the exception of yellow and gold stamping, did not look any better than the Doubleday issue. It was certainly no better than the Dodge one, which comparison McDonald does not make. As a matter of fact, Grosset merely took over remaining sheets of the last Dodge edition, and issued them in two ways: (1), using the Dodge cases, with Dodge on the backbone, but with Grosset and Dunlap on the title page; and (2), placing their own name on the backbone, as well as on the title page. McDonald says the Grosset edition is an interesting form for the collector to have. It is merely the remainder sheets of the second American edition bound cheaply with a reprint house's name on the title page. There were also copies printed and bound by Grosset and Dunlap after they had used up the Dodge sheets.

[6] JENNIE GERHARDT
New York, 1911

The first edition of this book exists in two issues as to binding. That much is admitted by McDonald, who says he is forced to leave the mystery unsolved. The two issues were long supposed identical as to sheets, the only variant being the stamping of the author's name on the backbone of the binding. Issue 1 had *Theodore / Dreiser*, and Issue 2 only *Dreiser*. Much controversy had arisen about which issue was the first, a great deal of the printed matter pertaining to it being merely hearsay. For example, the statement has been made that Dreiser objected to the use of only his surname on the backbone, on the theory that he was not well enough known to appear abbreviated before the public. He ordered that the binding be printed with both names, so the two-name issue must have been the second. Upon investigating this very logical theory, I could discover no evidence to substantiate it . . . in fact the publishers themselves have no recollection of any such incident. More important, Dreiser himself states that it was not so. In a letter from Dreiser dated September 13, he says "no" in answer to the question "Did you discover that these two cases were being used and request that only one be used." This seems to spike the theory for good. Yet this story was so plausible that it was generally accepted.

The one-name edition, as it has become known, has been called by other commentators, book dealers, and collectors, the first issue.

Everything pointed to the fact that this must be true. The one-name is by far the scarcest, so the conclusion was reached that an error had been made by the publishers in using only one name; after a few copies were bound the mistake was rectified. But the truth seems to run in the opposite direction. The one-name issue is *not* the first, and in fact the binding "point" is only half of it.

The first issue of JENNIE GERHARDT is that with the words *Theodore / Dreiser* stamped upon the spine of the binding, and with a typographical error on page 22, line eight from bottom, where there appears the word "IS" instead of "IT." I have a copy of this two-name issue before me. It was given by Harper and Brothers to Mr. Frederic Melcher, the well-known editor of *The Publisher's Weekly*, who was, in 1911, associated with Charles Lauriat and Company, the Boston booksellers. The book was sent to Mr. Melcher in advance of publication, according to the custom of the publishers. On the title page, there are stamped with a rubber stamp these words "Advance Copy—Not Published." Mr. Arthur Rushmore, head of the manufacturing department of Harper and Brothers, had declared that that firm was in the habit of mailing such advance copies to reviewers and bookmen, and in no conceivable way could they have mailed anything but the first issue. A presentation copy from Dreiser to Mr. Wm. C. Lengel, given the day before publication also has the two-name backbone. I concluded that this evidence of the two-name issue's priority was almost but not entirely conclusive.

I then read the one-name copy for typographical errors, and sent the two-name copy for a reading to Mr. Louis Feipel, of the Brooklyn Public Library, a specialist at spotting the most infinitesimal typographical error or broken letter. Mr. Feipel found 24 misprints, 40 broken letters, and 23 textual errors in fact and grammar. Strangely enough, all except one of these remained uncorrected in the one-name copy. Let me say here, that I do not subscribe to the so-called "broken-letter necromancy." Broken letters, from the fact that they might have been broken in the plate and corrected in printing, or that they might have been perfect in the first printing, and broken as printing continued, can be used by one man to prove one issue the first, and by another to prove his issue the first.

In the two-name issue, on page 22, in the eighth line from the bottom, the text reads, "she should use *is* for whatever she wants."

Turning to the same page in the one-name issue, we find that the word *is* has been removed from the plate, and corrected by insertion of the word *it*. The discovery of this correction ought to prove that the two-name issue was the first issue, but, I have examined a dozen or more copies of the two-name issue, in which the word *is* had been corrected to *it*. This is confusing enough, and seems to indicate that the one or two names on the binding makes no difference without the type correction. The mess can only be straightened out by considering what actually occurred in the publishing office of Harpers.

With the assistance of Mr. Arthur Rushmore and Mr. Eugene Reynal of Harpers and of Mr. E. J. Hirle, the man who printed the book, as well as Mr. Jas. MacNamee, the binder, and Mr. Joseph Harper, who was head of the manufacturing department of Harpers in 1911, the following came to light. First there were printed up a certain number of sheets of JENNIE GERHARDT, which were piled up ready to be bound. This number was gauged by what the publishers supposed the sale would be. It was Dreiser's second book, and he was, at that time, not a best seller in any sense of the word. The number, therefore, was not large. The binder was then ordered to make the binding or the cases and also "brass dies" to stamp them with. "Dies" are pieces of brass, upon which the letters are cut to form the title, and author's and publisher's name to be stamped upon the front cover and backbone of the binding. For the backbone, in this case, three "dies" were used: One for JENNIE GER-HARDT and an ornament at the top, one for *Theodore / Dreiser* in the middle, and one for *Harpers* at the bottom. The "dies" have to be cut by hand from drawing or type proof. Here the three "dies" were all exactly the same style of lettering, a thin serif letter very much like a Scotch-Roman type-face a little condensed. The fact to be emphasized is that the letters on the three "dies" matched. With these "dies," the backbone was stamped, and a number of cases, with the author's full name on the backbone, were delivered to Harpers. In these cases were placed the original sheets (with the error on page 22), and the finished book emerged. This was the first issue.

Now a certain number, probably a small one, of these original uncorrected sheets remained piled up and uncased for a while, as well as a number of two-name cases, because as often happens, the first orders did not come up to the number of sheets and cases on hand. Harpers had sent out the first issue to reviewers and to book men (Mr. Melcher got his then) and the book salesmen had got orders which were filled. After such initial activities in a publishing office, there always comes a lull when nothing happens. Everyone is waiting to see if the book takes on or dies. JENNIE GERHARDT, in a very little while took on. When this became apparent, Harpers recognized the need for a larger number of sheets than there were left from the first printing, so a new batch was ordered. At this point, it occurred to some one to read the first sheets, and on page 22, line eight from the bottom was discovered the error of *is* for *it*. Out of 24 misprints in that issue, this was the first and most serious. The moment it was discovered, the plate of page 22 was gouged out, and the word *it* inserted. Then the plate was put back in page order, the remaining incorrect sheets were destroyed, and a second larger batch of sheets printed. Notice that now all the original sheets are, in reality, done away with. Then the binders used the leftover cases (with the two-name backbone) to bind the new sheets that had the error on page 22 corrected. This accounts for the issue with *Theodore / Dreiser* on backbone having the error corrected in the text. Consequently, this is the second issue.

Now enter the villain! New cases were needed, but when the binders started to stamp them, they found that one of the dies was missing—the middle die on which had been cut the author's name *Theodore / Dreiser*. So a new die was hurriedly cut. One has to know the workings of the inside of a publisher's office to understand this. No one man follows a single book every minute from manuscript to delivery truck but, many men have a hand in it, each one doing a different job. Often these different men do not know in some books what has come before, or what comes after. In this case, the man who cut the new die for the author's name was either a new man, and not the one who cut the original die sometime before, or else he was the same man, making a mistake. Anyway, he cut only the word *Dreiser* this time. This die was locked into the form, and the backbone stamped with one name *Dreiser*. When these cases were ready, the binders started to pick up the sheets of the second printing and bind them in, so the one-name issue contains the sheets corrected. It is, getting down to fine points, the third issue of JENNIE GERHARDT.

Now, if the reader can come up for a breath a minute, the last phase of this mess may be gone into. Why, he will enquire, is the two-name issue more common than the one-name? A fair question . . . and it deserves an answer. The answer can be seen by glancing at the tabulation of these three issues of JENNIE GERHARDT.

First Issue: Two-name backbone with error on page 22 uncorrected.
Second Issue: Two-name backbone with error on page 22 corrected.
Third Issue: One-name backbone with error on page 22 corrected.

In other words, the first two issues are the same as to backbone but before the point of the error on page 22 was known, both these issues were grouped together without any distinction. Consequently they were together more numerous than the third issue with the one-name which was not done until after all the two-name originally ordered cases were used up.

The mottled blue cloth binding appeared in no subsequent issues, although the book was reprinted twice in 1911 which issues were bound in solid color blue cloth, and four times thereafter until Boni and Liveright took over the plates from Harpers in 1923. They brought it out under their imprint in May, 1924. A. L. Burt, the reprint house, issued the book in a copyright edition in March, 1924. There was published by P. Zsolnay, Berlin, Wein, Leipzig, in 1928, a German edition, under the title of JENNIE GERHARDT, *Roman. Die Ubers. aus. d. Engl. beforgte Alfons Matthias Neuse.* An English edition was brought out by Harpers in London, November, 1911.

[7] SISTER CARRIE
(The Harper Edition) *New York, 1912*

TITLE PAGE

SISTER CARRIE / A Novel / By / Theodore Dreiser / Author of / "Jennie Gerhardt" / (Publisher's device with motto) / Harper & Brothers Publishers / New York and London / MCMXII (Hair line rule box around first type line, another encloses second, third, fourth, fifth and sixth type lines and device, another encloses last three type lines. Another hair line box about the whole.)

PAGES

Preliminary pages (iv) plus 560 pages. Pages 1, and pages 558, 559, 560 unnumbered. Pages 558, 559, 560 blank. (i): Title page, as above. (verso):

Copyright, 1900, By Harper & Brothers / (rule) / Printed in the United States of America / Published February, 1912 / I-N (iii): Publisher's Note / (full page of text) (verso): Blank. Text: pp. (1)-557.

BINDING

Page size; 7 1/4 x 4 7/8; blue mottled cloth, front cover stamped in gold and ornament in dark blue ink; SISTER / CARRIE / (an ornament) / *Theodore Dreiser* Backbone stamped in gold as follows: SISTER / CARRIE / (an ornament) / *Theodore* / *Dreiser* / Harpers. Back cover blank. All edges trimmed. End papers white. Uniform with JENNIE GERHARDT, THE FINANCIER, and THE TITAN.

The Harper SISTER CARRIE belongs in a collector's set of Dreiser books since it is the first to carry an introduction. This part of the book, under the heading of "Publisher's Note," presents us with an interesting comment by his publisher upon Dreiser's standing as a novelist, and gives quotations from critics to this effect, all of which are worthy of preservation. The publishers explain that they deem SISTER CARRIE entitled to a "worthy format," so they put it in the library edition. There were 2500 copies of this edition printed. It was reprinted in 1913.

SISTER CARRIE was to pass through still another mutation before it arrived for good in the offices of Horace Liveright, its present publisher. Early in 1917, Mr. Frank Shay, the author, who was publisher of the poetry of Edna St. Vincent Millay, also became publisher of Theodore Dreiser. He took over the plates of SISTER CARRIE (veteran plates by this time) from Dreiser himself, who had owned them ever since the Doubleday first edition. There was a contract between the new publisher and Dreiser calling for the immediate publication of SISTER CARRIE and the implied reissuing of other Dreiser titles from the Harper and John Lane lists over the Shay imprint. Although the SISTER CARRIE plates had been resting in the John Lane office, and were delivered to Shay at Dreiser's order, there existed no contract between that firm and Mr. Shay. Mr. Shay immediately arranged with Vail Ballou, the book printers, to do an edition of SISTER CARRIE. This edition was on the press or in the binder's hands, Mr. Shay does not recall the exact stage, when he was compelled to relinquish his contract with Dreiser on account of the World War, in which this country had just entered. Mr. Shay then made Dreiser known to Horace Liveright, who took over the Dreiser-Shay contract for the firm of

Boni and Liveright. But, in the meantime, five copies of SISTER CARRIE were bound up especially for Mr. Shay, in his cases, with the title pages tipped in by hand. With the exception of a copy that was once owned by Mr. Alfred Goldsmith, the eminent Dreiser and Whitman collector, no copy of this Shay issue has ever come to light. Mr. Shay's personal library in Provincetown was raided by vandals in 1929, and the copies of SISTER CARRIE were taken. While this issue of five copies is, in no sense, a new edition, it is, nevertheless another issue. I have not felt like listing it as a requisite to a complete Dreiser collection, because, except the new publisher's name on the title page, it contained not an added line of print. But it is one of those extremely curious and ephemeral things that a collector likes to have, and of course it could, if the point were stretched, be included in a collection as evidence of the numerous issues that this first Dreiser book went through. When Boni and Liveright printed their first edition of SISTER CARRIE in July, 1917, its harried and varied career was ended. They continued to print it, I don't know how many times. It still sells.

[8] THE FINANCIER
New York, [1913]

This, the last Dreiser book to be actually published by the house of Harper, is a very simple problem for the collector. While not rare in the real sense of that word, it is, nevertheless, pretty scarce in fine condition. The blue mottled cloth faded quickly, and the leaf (not real gold) with which Harper's stamped all Dreiser's books turned green. To find a copy in pristine state is extremely difficult today. There were 6000 copies of the first edition. It was reprinted three times by Harpers, and bound in plain cloth. It was finally turned over to Boni and Liveright, who continue to print it. There was also a reprint edition from A. L. Burt in 1915.

On page 214 the ends of lines 1 and 2 are in some copies badly mashed. Plates often get dropped and damaged like this. Also pieces of foreign matter sometimes interfere with perfect printing leaving words or letters blank. Which happened in this case no one knows. Regardless, however, of the cause, no "issues" may be made out of this "point." Copies with these lines mashed may have been printed first, or on the other hand, they may have come off the press last.

Broken letters mean anything that one may wish to read into them.

Mr. H. L. Mencken, probably of all American critics, the most interested in Dreiser, contributed to the *N. Y. Times Book Review*, December, 1912 the best review in print of this book. Later, in January, 1913, he again discussed THE FINANCIER in *Smart Set*.

[9] A TRAVELER AT FORTY
New York, [1913]

There are two issues of the first edition of this, Dreiser's first book of non-fiction. Of the first edition 3000 sets of sheets were printed by The Century Company, the fifth publisher to enter the lists. After 2500 sets of sheets out of this 3000 had been bound, the binding was changed to a cloth of a slightly different shade of red, making the remaining 500 the second issue. The change was probably made through the inability of the publishers to match the cloth exactly. It is practically impossible to describe in words the difference between the two cloths, as it would be necessary to have them together to see the distinction. It would seem that the cloth binding of the first 2500 issued is of a somewhat more dullish, brick red color; while the binding of the second issue seems to be a red of a brighter shade with less of a yellow tinge. In the perfect bibliography of Dreiser, which someone will compile some day, the enterprising bibliographer may hit upon the notion of tipping in samples of the cloth of these two editions. That, indeed, is the only way in which the distinction may be demonstrated. The book was reprinted in January, 1914, September, 1914, January, 1920, and October, 1923, but the binding in these issues was different from the first two, and it was stamped in black ink. Boni and Liveright took over the book in sheets in June, 1926. The first English edition, published by Grant Richards, consisted of the small number of 260 copies brought out in May, 1914.

Only four periodical publications of the chapters that go to make up this book can be discovered. A TRAVELER AT FORTY may be said to have been written to order. Dreiser took his European trip as the guest of Grant Richards, the English publisher, and the book was the immediate result. It is unlikely that much more of the book appeared in magazines before its publication.

[10] THE TITAN
New York, [1914]

This book started off as a Harper publication. It was accepted, and printed from plates by Harpers to the number of 8500 sets of sheets. Here again conditions arose which caused Dreiser to seek another publisher, and he was made a free agent. The American branch of John Lane, the English publisher, under the direction of Mr. J. Jefferson Jones, was making a new tradition in American publishing about that time and to Mr. Jones Dreiser turned. THE TITAN plates, which Harpers had made were handed over to Lane, with the 8500 sets of sheets, and 4000 advance orders which had been placed with Harpers for the book. Lane published the book on May 15, 1914. The second edition, a month after the first, was bound in plain blue-grey cloth.

When Dodd, Mead became Dreiser's publishers, they took from John Lane 175 bound copies of THE TITAN, and 1250 sets of sheets. They never issued the book under their own imprint, however, for on January 25, 1923, they transferred an assignment of copyright on this book to Dreiser. The bound copies and sheets were transferred to Boni and Liveright, who had just become Dreiser's publishers.

The English edition of March 5, 1915, was made from 1500 sets of sheets imported by the John Lane office from the American branch. In July, 1928, John Constable, publisher, brought out what they called "the new uniform edition" of THE TITAN.

A comprehensive review of this book written by Mr. H. L. Mencken appeared in *Smart Set* for August, 1914. It was less than a year later, April 17, 1915, that Randolph Bourne took occasion to sum up Dreiser's work as a novelist in *The New Republic*.

[11] LIFE IN A GARRISON TOWN
by Lieut. Bilse, *New York, 1914*

This book is a very interesting, important, and comfortably scarce item belonging to a Dreiser collection. It marks the first appearance of Dreiser as the author of an introduction to another man's book. The history of the book itself is an engrossing one, but too long to insert here. Suffice to say it was a very popular "exposé" of conditions in the German Army, and being published first in America in 1904 by Frederick A. Stokes, it went through ten editions in the next ten years. Several of these editions had points of difference, as to prefaces and introductions by other hands. But it was only to the tenth edition, issued by Lane at the beginning of the World War (after the book had been out of print for some time) that Dreiser contributed an introduction. The sale of this edition, so Mr. Jones states, was disappointing, and it was not put to press again. The appearance of Dreiser in this one edition only, accounts for its existence not being mentioned by any previous bibliographer, as well as for its scarcity. It will undoubtedly become one of the rare items in a Dreiser set. A part of its collation follows:

TITLE PAGE

LIFE IN A / GARRISON TOWN / The Military Novel / Suppressed By The / German Government / By Lieutenant Bilse / The Authorized Translation of / "Aus Einer Kleinen Garnison" / With A Foreword By Theodore / Dreiser, An introduction By / Arnold White / And A Summary of The Court-Martial / New York: John Lane Company / London: John Lane, The Bodley Head / MCMXIV

First 5 lines enclosed by double rule box, 6th line ditto, lines 7-13 inclusive, ditto; lines 14-16 inclusive, ditto; Whole surrounded by single rule box.

Verso of Title Page: Copyright, 1904 / By John Lane / Tenth Edition The foreword by Dreiser occupied pages (v) to (xiii) inclusive. The book when first published in The United States by Frederick A. Stokes had the date "January 1904" on copyright page and an introduction by Wolf Von Schierbrand. John Lane first published an edition in this country in March 1904 which had a portrait, and a prefatory note unsigned.

[12] THE "GENIUS"
New York, 1915

The "GENIUS," it may be said, is as much of an English publication as it is an American. Soon after Dreiser had submitted the MS of the book to the American office of John Lane Co. Mr.

Frederick Chapman, literary advisor to the London office, happened to be in New York so took the occasion to read it. He advised acceptance. While Mr. J. Jefferson Jones was arranging terms and contracts with Dreiser, Mr. Chapman returned to England and Mr. Jones sent him the MS. There Mr. Chapman, at Dreiser's request, cut out about 50,000 words, returned the MS to Mr. Jones in New York who put it to press. As the book was set up, it was found still to be too lengthy. Another cut was arranged. At the suggestion of Dreiser, Mr. Floyd Dell, the novelist and poet, was retained to delete even more pages from THE "GENIUS." He sliced out about 100 pages in proof so that in the end the book, a mere shadow of its original form, got between covers. About 11,000 sets of sheets were printed on bulking paper. 9190 sets of sheets were bound up in America. The remaining 1810 sets of sheets were taken back by the London office together with 400 bound copies, both going to make up the English edition, which is scarcer than the American.

It may, therefore, be stated that the first edition of this book, as to printing, was the same for both American and English branches of John Lane . . . the only difference being in the binding and staining of the top edges. The "point" of the numeral being misplaced on page 497, (see McDonald) may or may not be important . . . it occurs in both the American and English issues. If the collector wishes to get the actual first issue in point of time, he will be in a quandary to decide between the American and English issues. This is enough to make the English issue important, but also one must consider that it was the book widely circulated and read even in this country during the "suppression" of the American publication. The collector should have both issues, then there will be no question about it.

For these reasons I feel it wise to include a collation of the English issue as to binding. It will be noticed that this has wine colored stained tops, while, on the contrary, the distinction to be observed in the first American is the plain white edges all around. The staining was done, of course, after the sheets had been bound. Another "point" to be taken into consideration is the actual thickness of the sheets of the bound book. They will measure, in the first state (English and American the same) about one quarter inch thicker than copies of the second state. The bulking paper after the first printing was changed, accounting for this discrepancy.

7 7/8 inches x 5 3/8 inches. Wine red woven cloth, top edges trimmed and stained wine red, other edges white uncut.

FRONT COVER

Blind stamped boxes made up of six 2 point rules vertical and six horizontal . . . the inside four being double rules. In each of the four corners made by juxtaposition of rules, is a blind stamped flower ornament. In the center box is blind stamped THE "GENIUS" / Theodore / Dreiser

BACKBONE

Stamped in gold leaf (two point double rule) / (blind stamped flower ornament) / (Another rule same size) / THE / "GENIUS" / Theodore / Dreiser / The Bodley Head / (another double rule) / (another blind stamped ornament) / (another double rule) Box of one point blind stamped rule around type lines.

The American edition of THE "GENIUS" published in October, 1915, was widely sold up to the summer of 1916. Some time in the month of July, a representative of the *New York Society For The Prevention of Vice* walked into the offices of the John Lane Co. He told Mr. Jones that his organization had received so many complaints from high minded persons about THE "GENIUS" that some action would have to be initiated. The representative was none other than Mr. John Sumner, Secretary of the Society, who declared that personally he thought the book rather a fine piece of literature. Nevertheless, certain persons had raised a row and something must be done to appease them. That, in point of fact, was what the Society existed for.

Then, another person, a Mr. Rowe, secretary of a similar band in Cincinnati, had decided that THE "GENIUS" was not a fit work for the great American public to read. He got up and circulated a letter amongst the postoffice inspectors in all English speaking countries, carefully selecting and calling attention to the "75 lewd and 17 profane passages" that Dreiser had seen fit to put into the book.

Another person, a Major Funkhauser, a spokesman for the comstocks of Chicago, was also active in swinging public opinion against THE "GENIUS."

The appeal of Mr. Rowe to the Federal postoffice inspectors, made, obviously, in hopes that it would result in barring the book from the United States post, came to nothing. A Federal representative called on Mr. Jones in the Lane offices, but after being shown the many favorable reviews of THE "GENIUS" and after some talk, he, evidently being a man of sense, went away. The book was never bothered by the Government authorities.

But Mr. Sumner and others of his stamp were active enough to intimidate Lane into withdrawing the book after it had been sold in great numbers for about nine months. This result (though somewhat *ex post facto*) of the comstockian activities was enough to arouse a sense of justice and liberty in a large group of people naturally opposed to bigotry and intolerance. Numerous groups protested officially and informally. McDonald, in his book, lists and prints several of these arresting protests in shape of telegrams and broadsides. Many people were stirred to speeches and debates and, in the end, court proceedings finished off the case. The curious may read the complete story of the legal aspects in a pamphlet by Mr. Elias Rosenthal, entitled *Theodore Dreiser's "Genius" Damned*. In the *North American Review* for June, 1918 was a piece by Mr. Joseph S. Auerbach, the attorney who handled the case, which article was entitled *Authorship and Liberty—Argument Before The Appelate Division of The Supreme Court in The Suppression of The "Genius."* An account of the case also appeared in the current newspapers and in the law journals.

After Lane, under Mr. Sumner's pressure, had stopped selling THE "GENIUS" in America, the remaining stock of the book was shipped to England where it was sold. Dreiser, in instituting a suit against the John Lane Co. for not selling his book, seemed to contend, with some logic it must be admitted, that Lane should do one of two things: either sell the book or the contract. For a while neither was done. By 1923 Lane passed over the contract as well as the contracts of the other Dreiser books on their list to Dodd, Mead. As a matter of fact, Lane not only sold Dreiser's books, but withdrew altogether from publishing in America and were taken over as a company by Dodd, Mead. On February 3, 1923, the last named firm had caused to be transferred them by Lane, the rights to THE "GENIUS" and THE BULWARK. This all occurred, it may be well to

remark, eight years after Lane had published the last Dreiser book to
bear their imprint (A HOOSIER HOLIDAY) and six years after Boni
and Liveright first appeared on the title page of FREE AND OTHER
STORIES. It was only six months later that Boni and Liveright published THE "GENIUS" in a new edition with an introduction (see
page 49).

During the period that Dodd, Mead owned rights to THE
"GENIUS," there was some talk of Mr. H. L. Mencken revising the
book so that it would not be in any danger of Mr. Sumner's stric-
tures. Fortunately nothing ever came of it.

Some sort of jinx evidently laid hold of THE "GENIUS" for from
the time it was a MS until it became a book and had been on the mar-
ket for nine months, it was hexed in one way or another.

Before it got to be a book at all it was cut down twice by different hands, as I have related. When it was accepted by *The
Metropolitan Magazine* to be run in parts as a serial, it was submitted to still another operation. Mr. William Lengel, associated
with Dreiser on the Butterick Publications, rewrote the book and
made a 100,000 word version to fit the needs of *The Metropolitan.*

In October, 1928 Constable in London published THE "GENIUS"
in a new uniform edition.

[13] PLAYS OF THE NATURAL AND THE SUPERNATURAL
New York, 1916

John Lane published the first edition in 1916. (See McDonald)
When Dodd, Mead took over the John Lane Co. they obtained
the rights to Dreiser's books but apparently only one, PLAYS OF THE
NATURAL AND THE SUPERNATURAL, was ever published under the
Dodd, Mead imprint. On April 21, 1922, they printed an edition
of 500 copies; in May of the same year 248 sets of sheets were
bound up and later in June, 3 sets more were bound, making a
total of 251 bound books actually published by this firm. On
February 2, 1923, they sold the remaining 249 unbound sheets to
Dreiser. In the Dodd, Mead edition the appendix "*An Anæsthetic
Revelation*" formed a part of the signature. Dreiser probably turned
the sheets over to Boni and Liveright as he did others. Copies of the
Dodd, Mead issue may hardly be considered as a new edition but

only a new impression for the only text changes in the book were Dodd, Mead's name on the title page and the new dates there and on verso.

In the 1916 Lane edition (the first) there were seven plays. But when Boni and Liveright published this book on Dec. 18, 1926, two other plays, *Phatasmagoria* and *The Court of Progress*, which originally appeared in the first edition of HEY RUB-A-DUB-DUB, were included in a special edition of 12 copies which were all sent to Europe. It had been planned to include in this edition *The Dream*, from HEY RUB-A-DUB-DUB, thus making all together three more plays in this edition to go abroad, but by oversight *The Dream* was omitted. To rectify the error still another edition of ten copies was then made up and published on December 28, 1926. This included all three plays above mentioned. These editions are interesting but can not be termed in any way first editions of anything. Copies are only necessary to a complete collection of Dreiserana in the sense that they are curious forms. All the plays had appeared, of course, in book form before. The reason why the two very limited editions were made up at all was because an opportunity had arisen to submit Dreiser's plays to a European play producer.

In some copies of the original first Lane edition 1916, there are tipped in back sheets entitled *An Anæsthetic Revelation*. It may be said that as these were placed in the book *after* it had been printed (Mr. Dreiser states this to be a fact) a second issue was created. On the other hand it may be maintained, looking at it from a more technical point of view, that this was another edition. Collectors, one believes, will want both states . . . without the tipped-in sheets for the first state and with them for the second state.

John Lane Co., the London publishers, imported from America 250 bound copies of PLAYS which they put out as the English Edition in 1916.

Following is a list of the plays and the periodicals where they first appeared.

"*The Girl in the Coffin*" ....*Smart Set*, October 1913
"*The Blue Sphere*" ....*Smart Set*, December 1914
"*Laughing Gas*" ....*Smart Set*, February 1915
"*In The Dark*" ....*Smart Set*, January 1915
"*The Spring Recital*" ....*The Little Review*, December 1915
"*The Light In The Window*"...........................*The International*, January 1916

[14] THE BULWARK
New York, 1916

Here is an item which few collectors have ever seen or will see. And no wonder. From the nature of the thing, no one would have had occasion to save any, for who saves dummies. Further no more than a hundred copies, if as many, could have been made and that was fourteen years ago. I only know of one actual specimen of this item and have never heard nor seen any others. The copy examined was given to Mr. W. W. Lange who in turn gave it to Morton Hiscox, with whose kind permission I reproduce it here. Because of the inscription in Dreiser's holograph, it is Mr. Hiscox's opinion that possibly only one copy was made up and that to show to Dreiser. This of course would make it an edition of one copy and so rare that no collector could hope ever to own one. As a matter of fact, THE BULWARK was never really published nor the MS ever finished.

The description given here applies to a "dummy" printed and bound by John Lane in 1916 for sales purposes. As was their custom, according to Mr. Jones, about 100 copies of such dummies were made up before the book was manufactured, and given out to salesmen or otherwise distributed to the trade. The publication date of THE BULWARK was announced several times, but for various reasons the book never reached that stage. Lane advertised it would be "the greatest novel that has ever been written," and in a brochure further advertised it to be ready in "the spring of 1917." Later, when Boni and Liveright took over Dreiser's books from Dodd, Mead, they also advertised THE BULWARK in a brochure announcing it would be ready for publication in 1920. Dreiser himself was writing as late as March 17, 1920*** "I hope to have THE BULWARK finished and published yet this year***." But evidently he never did for it certainly never was published. The book was to deal with the struggle of the head of a Quaker family to bring up his children in the orthodox fashion and with the influence of modern society upon these children's beliefs and actions. It is too bad Dreiser never finished it for here he was concerned with at least a new locale.

This item is certainly an important one to Dreiser collectors regardless of how one feels about it being a book. The fact remains that here for the first and only time appears in print, between

THE BULWARK

BY

THEODORE DREISER

NEW YORK: JOHN LANE COMPANY
LONDON: JOHN LANE, THE BODLEY HEAD
TORONTO: S. B. GUNDY :: MCMXVI

boards, 9 pages of Dreiser which have never appeared anywhere else. It is the most unique and curious of all Dreiser items, though it be neither flesh, fish nor fowl. It is, too, the rarest since only one copy is known.

TITLE PAGE

THE / BULWARK / By / Theodore Dreiser / New York; John Lane Company / London: John Lane. The Bodley Head / Toronto: S. B. Gundy; MCMXVI.

PAGES

Preliminary pages (vi) plus 16. (i) Half Title; The Bulwark. (Verso): By Theodore Dreiser / (a double rule) / The "Genius" / Sister Carrie / Jennie Gerhardt / A Traveler at Forty / Plays Of The Natural and The Supernatural / (a dotted line) / A Trilogy of Desire / 1. The Financier / 2. The Titan / 3.******/ (A double rule). (iii): Title-page, as above. (Verso): Copyright, 1916, / By John Lane Company / Press of / J. J. Little & Ives Company / New York, U.S.A. (v): Half-title, The Bulwark (Verso): Blank. pp 7-16 text. pp 17-? blank.

BINDING

8 x 5 1/2 inches. Bound in green ribbed cloth stamped in gold. All edges cut.

FRONT COVER

The Bulwark / (a rule) / Theodore Dreiser (facsimile of his signature). Whole enclosed in box of single rule. Stamped on gold background rectangle 2 1/8 x 4 1/2 in.

BACKBONE

The / Bulwark / (a rule) / Dreiser / John Lane / Company

[15] A HOOSIER HOLIDAY
New York, 1916

Apart from the original page 173 which this book must have to be a first issue, it must also have a green buckram backbone. The blue buckram backbone belongs to another issue. The book never went into a second printing while Lane had it. As copies were needed for the trade the sheets were bound up which accounts for variant in backbone. Dodd, Mead took over from John Lane 950 sewn sheets of A HOOSIER HOLIDAY. Of this number, they bound

42

up 251 in their cases. This makes still another issue of the book. There is no record existing to indicate whether Dodd, Mead sold these books or whether they disposed of them before copies reached the public. Certainly no copy has come to light yet. On February 2, 1923 they sold the remaining 699 sheets to Dreiser. Boni and Liveright, in the same year, obtained these sheets from Dreiser and bound them into an edition which they issued in September, 1925 using plain blue buckram cases stamped in gold.

This is apparently the only Dreiser book of non-fiction chapters of which were not published first in periodicals.

[16] THE BEST SHORT STORIES OF 1916
Boston, [1917]

See McDonald page 77. Contains first appearance of "The Lost Phoebe" in book form. No date on title page of this book.

[17] LIFE, ART AND AMERICA
New York, [1917]

See McDonald pp 49-50. This pamphlet, when originally published, sold for 25 cents. Today it sells for one hundred times that. Many collectors are finding that the bound copies of the magazine *The Seven Arts* where this piece first appeared are worth having in a Dreiser collection. It was a periodical, the conduct of which, Dreiser had a deal to do with. These bound copies of *The Seven Arts* seem about as scarce, if not scarcer than the separate pamphlet printed from it.

[18] FREE AND OTHER STORIES
New York, 1918

This collection contained the most popular of all the Dreiser ventures into the short story form, *"The Lost Phoebe."* Below are listed the first and subsequent appearances of this story as well as of others in the book.

"Free" ....*The Saturday Evening Post*, March
16, 1918. Illustrated by F. F. Gruger.
A BOOK OF LONG STORIES, New York, 1927

"*McEwen of The Shining Slave Makers*" ....*Ainslee's*, June, 1901 as "The Shining Slave Makers."
"*Nigger Jeff*" ....*Ainslee's*, November, 1901
"*The Lost Phoebe*" ....*The Century Magazine*, April, 1916
THE BEST SHORT STORIES OF 1916, Boston, [1917]
GREAT AMERICAN SHORT STORIES, New York, 1920
REPRESENTATIVE AMERICAN SHORT STORIES, New York, 1923
GREAT SHORT STORIES OF THE WORLD, New York, 1925
Famous Stories Magazine, May 1926
AMERICAN MYSTERY STORIES, New York, 1927
"*The Second Choice*" ....*Cosmopolitan*, February, 1918 as "Second Choice"
CONTEMPORARY SHORT STORIES Boston, 1926
AMERICAN LITERATURE, New York, 1926
"*Old Rogaum and His Theresa*" ....*Reedy's Mirror*, Dec. 12, 1901 as "Butcher Rogaum's Door."
CENTURY READINGS IN THE AMERICAN SHORT STORY, New York, 1927
"*The Cruise of The 'Idlewild'* " ....*The Bohemian Magazine*, October 1909
"*Married*" ....*The Cosmopolitan*, Sept. 1917
"*When The Old Century Was New*" ....*Pearson's*, January 1901 as "When The Old Century Was New; A Love Story" illustrated.

[19] FREE AND OTHER STORIES
New York, [1918]

The first edition of this book with an introduction by Sherwood Anderson was published by The Modern Library when that group of books was owned by Boni and Liveright. The first issue had the device or mark of Boni and Liveright on the title page. Later editions, after The Modern Library was sold to Mr. Bennett Cerf and Mr. Donald Klopfer, had the new device of The Modern Library on title page.

[20] THE HAND OF THE POTTER
New York, 1918

The arresting fact about this book is revealed by an examination of the date and the actual copyright records. The date on the title page as on the copyright page reads *1918*, yet the date of publication was September 20, 1919 and of copyright Sept. 27, 1919. The book was manufactured in 1918 but on account of its postponement for play production (as related by McDonald) it was not sent to the copyright office until the following year. During the period it was held up something must have happened to the preliminary sheet (iii-iv) for in some copies that sheet is neatly tipped in while in others it forms part of the signature.

No one in the publishing offices of Horace Liveright remembers what happened and no records are available to show the reason for the tip-in. Dreiser states that he knows nothing about this tip-in. One may assume from this, that the whole business, due to exigency of manufacture, occurred in the offices of Horace Liveright. Nevertheless, the theory as originally suggested by John T. Winterich, is substantiated by Mr. Thomas Smith, head of Horace Liveright, Inc., who says it could have occurred in no other fashion. The theory is this:

After the book was printed and bound in 1918, some error was discovered either on page (iii) which had the half-title, or more likely on page (iv) which had a list of Dreiser's books. It must have been a serious error for no publisher would go to the bother and expense of tearing out one sheet and printing and tipping in a new one for a minor reason. But whatever the error was or how serious, the publishers did take out the offending sheet and print up and tip-in a new one. Because no copies have ever come to light showing any errors on this sheet in question we can only assume that every copy of the first state was caught and the sheet removed. We may further assume that this first issue is non-existent, for in truth, it was made into another issue by the tipped-in sheet. Copies having the sheet tipped-in may be said, then, to belong to the first issue of the first edition.

When the bound copies thus corrected were exhausted, and new copies needed, the correction was made this time by actually printing a new signature or entirely new sheets for the book. This fact seems apparent because the text, on both sides of sheet iii-iv, is precisely the same in the copies with the tipped-in sheet as in copies with that sheet forming part of the signature. The broken letter "N" on page (iv) on the tipped in sheet occurs also on the bound-in sheet. Both were printed from same plates, indicating more clearly the procedure described above. It seems conclusive that the copies having the sheet part of the signature are copies of the second issue.

When the second binding was made, slight changes also occurred upon it. The lettering on the front cover and label of shelf-back were made from a hand-drawing. In some copies the style of this hand lettering differs somewhat, indicating that another binding was ordered, but the attempt to match the first was not perfectly successful.

It is unfortunate, in the case of THE HAND OF THE POTTER that the facts relating to its mutations can not be assembled. Records in forms of binding and printing orders, letters, etc., must conceivably exist in the offices of the publisher.

In addition to the regular trade first edition of this book, there were also a few copies, probably 25 or so, signed by Dreiser on the title page. These copies were taken from the trade edition, and were sold, by the publishers, (so I am told by Mr. David Moss, who bought some) for $5. each. They may be considered as association items of course, but in no wise as a limited or separate edition.

[21] TWELVE MEN
New York, 1919

The following chapters of TWELVE MEN first appeared in periodicals listed below:

"A Doer of The Word"	*Ainslee's*, June 1902. *Famous Stories Magazine*, Sept. 1926. SAMPLES, New York, 1928
"My Brother Paul"	Parts of this chapter were incorporated into the introduction written by Dreiser for *The Songs of Paul Dresser*, 1927 LITTLE BLUE BOOK, No. 660
"The Country Doctor"	*Harper's Monthly Magazine*, July 1918.
"A True Patriarch"	*McClure's Magazine.* December, 1907
"The Village Feudists"	*Famous Stories Magazine*, December, 1926
"The Mighty Rourke"	*McClure's Magazine*, May 1911 as "The Mighty Burke"
"A Mayor and His People"	*The Era Magazine*, June, 1903
"W. L. S."	*Harper's Weekly.* Dec. 14, 1901 as "Color of Today" LITTLE BLUE BOOK No. 660

[22] "HEY RUB-A-DUB-DUB"
New York, 1920.

The actual publication date should be January 15, 1920, instead of December, 1919. Several chapters were first published in magazines and some later used in books. Such a compilation follows:

"Hey Rub-A-Dub-Dub"	*The Nation*, August 30, 1919. THE NEW WORLD: COLLEGE READINGS IN ENGLISH. New York, 1920
"Some Aspects of Our National Character"	LITTLE BLUE BOOK No. 661
"The Dream"	*The Seven Arts Magazine*, July, 1917 (Dreiser had a hand in founding and conducting this magazine)
"Neurotic America and The Sex Impulse"	LITTLE BLUE BOOK No. 661
"Marriage and Divorce"	*The Forum*, July, 1920
"Life, Art and America"	*The Seven Arts*, February, 1917

Mr. McDonald remarks that HEY RUB-A-DUB-DUB is the shortest route to the Dreiserian view of life. In this connection it is interesting to note what H. L. Mencken wrote in *Smart Set*, March 15, 1920, when reviewing the book.

> "***There comes a time in every sentient man's life when he must simply unload his ideas, or burst***. In every line of HEY RUB-A-DUB-DUB there is evidence of the author's antecedent agony***The result is*** solemn stuff, with never a leer of beauty in it—in fact, almost furious.*** Is it good stuff? My feeling is that it isn't. More, my feeling is that Dreiser is no more fitted to do a book of speculation than Joseph Conrad, say, is fitted to do a college yell. His talents simply do not lie in that direction. He lacks the mental agility, the insinuating suavity, the necessary capacity for romanticizing a syllogism. Ideas themselves are such sober things that a sober man had better let them alone.***"

[23] CAIUS GRACCHUS
By Odin Gregory. *New York*, [1920]

See McDonald page 77. Odin Gregory is a pseudonym for someone, but for whom, it is not permitted to reveal.

[24] JURGEN AND THE CENSOR
New York, 1920

This is a pamphlet with the sub-title *"Report Of The Emergency Committee Organized to Protest Against The Suppression of James Branch Cabell's* JURGEN." It was privately printed at New York in 1920 and limited to 458 copies which were numbered. The Dreiser material therein consists of a statement made by Dreiser regarding JURGEN. This item is of some significance because it is a fine example of one American author's opinion about another, linked in this case by the fact that both were in trouble with the censors more than once.

[25] NOTICE
No date.

This piece of paper, 2 white sheets measuring 12 by 8 7/8 inches, printed on one side, is one of the most curious things in the long list of Dreiserana. It was issued by Dreiser to exonerate himself in an attack made upon him by one Annie Nathan Meyer. She had been associated with him whilst he was managing editor of *The Broadway Magazine*. Her attack took the form of a letter to *The Review*, April 30, 1920. Dreiser first reprints her letter, then prints his own in reply. His was dated Los Angeles, May 16, 1920. There is no knowing how many of these broadsides were printed or how many distributed, but probably not many. I have seen only two copies during the four years I have been hunting down Dreiserana.

[26] A BOOK ABOUT MYSELF
New York, [1922]

The first edition of this volume consisted of 1500 copies. Collectors should not be misled by the mis-spelling of the name Hearst as Heart on page 468, line 27. This error had been mentioned as a point. Yet, it appeared, as a matter of fact, in subsequent editions. Obviously, it means nothing.

Dreiser said in a letter in 1922 that he had finished two volumes of a three volume autobiography. A BOOK ABOUT MYSELF is unquestionably the first of this trilogy. The only parts of it one can find appearing in magazines are contained in a series published in *The Bookman*. The series was headed *Out of My Newspaper Days* and it ran from November, 1921 through to April, 1922 . . . five articles. In referring to these articles Dreiser said in another letter; "These in the *Bookman* were more excerpts from some chapters in a large volume already done. And that volume is only volume two

of a series of four volumes, concerning myself, three of which
have been completed. They will be issued one of these days when
the spirit moves me. At present they are lying in a trunk awaiting
a more favorable day." This was also written in 1922.

This first volume in which Dreiser revealed (in continued narra-
tive) something of his own early struggles, was well and widely
reviewed. Amongst the important periodicals noticing it were *The
Bookman*, Dec., 1922; *N. Y. Times Book Review*, Dec. 24, 1922;
Boston Transcript, Dec. 30, 1922; *N. Y. Tribune*, Dec. 31, 1922;
The Independent, Jan. 6, 1923; *The Literary Review*, Jan. 20,
1923; *The Smart Set*, March, 1923. Amongst the critics writing
about A BOOK ABOUT MYSELF were, to name a few, E. F. Edgett,
H. L. Mencken, Burton Rascoe, Edmund Lester Pearson, Joseph
Wood Krutch, and Richard Le Gallienne.

[27] THE "GENIUS"
New York, [*1923*]

After THE "GENIUS" had lain under the ban for seven years,
(because of the "suppression" and the suit) Boni and Liveright published it in a new edition in September, 1923, with an unsigned
preface. In their first two printings of the book, the authorship of
this preface was not acknowledged in type. It had been written by
Mr. Merton S. Yewdale (now editor-in-chief for E. P. Dutton)
who had published it in the *New York Sun*. When Mr. Yewdale
became aware that Boni and Liveright were issuing THE "GENIUS"
with his piece as a preface and not giving him credit, he brought it
to their attention. In the third issue under the Boni and Liveright
imprint, Mr. Yewdale's name appeared as the author. Since then,
the book has been reprinted over a dozen times. The collector will
require this book in the first printing with the unsigned preface,
that being the first issue of THE "GENIUS" with an introduction. If
more meticulous care as to issues need be recognized, the third with
Mr. Yewdale's name appearing, will also be found in a collection.

[28] THE COLOR OF A GREAT CITY
New York, [*1923*]

The first edition was of 3780 copies. All subsequent printings
are so noted on copyright page. There must be a great deal larger

number of first periodical appearances of parts of this book than can be found. Complete files of *Demorests*, *Era*, *The Puritan*, *The Ledger Monthly* and *The Voice* might reveal them. Unfortunately such files are non-existent so far as is known.

"The Log of a Harbor Pilot"	*Ainslee's*; July, 1899, as "The Log of An Ocean Pilot."
"The Flight of Pigeons"	*The Bohemian*; October, 1909
"The Track Walker"	*Tom Watson's Magazine*; June, 1905
"The Realization of An Ideal"	*Tom Watson's Magazine*; 1905
"When The Sails Are Furled"	*Ainslee's*. December 1898. Revised as "When The Sails Are Furled, Sailors Snug Harbor!"
"A Certain Oil Refinery"	AMERICAN ECONOMIC LIFE, by Tugwell, Munroe and Stryker. New York, 1925. Contains on pages 198-204 parts of this chapter.
"The Men In The Dark"	*The American Magazine*; Feb., 1912
"The Cradle of Tears"	*Tom Watson's Magazine*; May, 1905
"Whence The Song"	*Harper's Weekly*; Dec. 8, 1900
"Christmas in The Tenements"	*Harper's Weekly*; Dec. 6, 1902
"The Rivers of The Nameless Dead"	*Tom Watson's Magazine*; March, 1905
"Six o'Clock"	"1910." The magazine carried the year as its title. It was edited by the artist C. D. Falls and only appeared that one year.

[29] THE BEST SHORT STORIES OF 1923.
Boston, [1923]

Covered by McDonald on page 78.

[30] EBONY AND IVORY
By Llewellyn Powys. *New York, 1923*

The first edition was published by the American Library Service not Harcourt, Brace as McDonald states.

[31] DOUZE HOMMES
Paris, 1923

The first French translation was published in March 1923, at Paris by F. Rieder et Cie. It was translated by M. Fernande Helie. The first edition consisted of 336 copies; 6 of which were on Hollande

Van Gelder paper carrying numeration A to F and marked "Not for Sale;" 30 were on the same paper and numbered 1-30, and 300 were printed on antique laid stock and numbered 31-300. Copies of the last named issue are bound in light tan paper covers, printed with brown ink . . . altogether a very attractive volume. This is the first Dreiser book to be translated into French and published. The title page reads as follows;

Les Prosateurs Etranges Modernes / Theodore Dreiser / Douze Hommes / Traduit de l' Anglais / par Fernande Hélie / Edition originale / (ornament) / Paris / F. Rieder et Cie, Editeurs / 7, Place Saint-Sulpice, 7 / MCMXXIII

[32] LEONARDO
   [New York,] 1924-1925

This annual of the Leonardo da Vinci Art School was issued for the year 1924-1925. It is a 132 page book bound in grey wrappers with a picture of Mona Lisa pasted on the front cover. It was edited by Mr. Onorio Ruotolo and Miss Francesca Vinci Roman with the intention of issuing it every year. This number, however, was the only one that ever appeared. About 3000 copies were printed. Page 54 contained the poem *The Great Blossom* and a portrait of Dreiser. This poem later appeared in MOODS, CADENCED AND DECLAIMED. The book measured 12 1/2 by 9 1/2 inches. A good deal of the text of this volume is printed in the Italian language.

[33] THESE UNITED STATES; A SYMPOSIUM
   New York, [1924]

See McDonald page 78.

[34] AN AMERICAN TRAGEDY
   New York, 1925

To be added to any comment upon this book is the fact, undisputed this time, that the trade edition, correctly described by McDonald, pages 63-66, appeared a month or so before the more elaborate and pretentious limited and signed issue. Only one conclusion can be drawn from this and that is; the collector seeking the first edition will take the trade issue. The book was published December 14, 1925 and had 18,200 copies in the first edition. Both volumes were enclosed in a grey board slip case with a cover made with yellow printed label.

Early in 1927 the book was held to be obscene and tending to corrupt the morals of the young, and it was suppressed in Boston by Boston comstockery acting through the power and person of the police and *The Watch and Ward Society* there. Boni and Liveright sent Mr. Donald Friede (then vice-president of the company, now of Covici-Friede) to fight the case. On April 22, 1927 he appeared in the Municipal Court at Boston and was fined $100 for having sold a copy of the book to Captain George Peterson of the Boston police force. Lieutenant Hines of the same force testified that the book had not corrupted his morals. The case was appealed to the Superior Court by the publisher's lawyers, Mr. Clarence Darrow and Mr. Arthur Garfield Hays.

Mr. Morris Ernst's book To The Pure has some very pertinent allusions to the censorship exercised over The American Tragedy, as well as to its suppression by the *Watch and Ward Society* in Boston. He quotes George Bernard Shaw's masterful epigram about the stupid censorship of books. This is too good to be left out of any notes on The American Tragedy. Shaw says, "Censorship ends in logical completeness when nobody is allowed to read any books except the books nobody can read." Mr. Ernst goes on to say that American authors are so used to censorship nowadays that they are no longer troubled with it. He writes that "Dreiser refused to be perturbed any longer when the *Watch and Ward Society* swore out a warrant against The American Tragedy and departed for a vacation in Europe."

The American Tragedy was dramatized by Mr. Patrick Kearny and produced by Mr. Horace Liveright, in New York City.

In 1927 in connection with publicity for the book, Boni and Liveright offered a prize of $500 for the best essay to be entitled *"Was Clyde Griffiths Guilty of Murder in the First Degree?"* The prize was won by Prof. Albert H. Levitt, Prof. of Law at the Washington and Lee University, Lexington, Virginia.

Three pieces of interesting Dreiserana are concerned with this prize contest. A—Boni and Liveright first issued four pages of typewritten copy on white paper announcing the contest with details and conditions. These four pages were stapled together and issued without wrappers. B—When the contest had been won and the prize awarded to Prof. Levitt, his essay was issued in a 12 page stamped and typewritten folder . . . and bound in tan paper covers. On the front cover of the wrappers the following appeared: ESSAY No. 10, Submitted November 22, 1926. / WAS CLYDE GRIFFITHS GUILTY / OF MURDER IN THE FIRST DEGREE? / Albert Levitt / Lexington, Va. / November 15, 1926. C—At the same time Boni and Liveright issued a printed one sheet broadside entitled ANNOUNCING THE WINNER OF THE / ESSAY CONTEST ON THEODORE DREISER'S / AN AMERICAN TRAGEDY / (Text) / Boni and Liveright.

[35] THE MAN MENCKEN
By Isaac Goldberg   *New York, 1925*

See McDonald, page 79. Read "Published in October, 1925," on verso of title-page.

[36] CONTEMPORARY SHORT STORIES
Edited by Kenneth Allan Robinson   *New York and Boston, 1926*

See McDonald, page 79.

[37] LILITH
By George Sterling   *New York, 1926*

This book contained an introduction by Dreiser. One of Sterling's last books before his untimely death, it was published by The Macmillan Company, in an edition of only 1500 copies and is now out of print and moderately scarce.

[38] MOODS, CADENCED AND DECLAIMED
New York, 1926

This is one of the rare cases where the limited signed and numbered edition was brought out before the trade edition. It is the first and only edition since the trade edition appeared revised. Below are all of the poems found first appearing in periodicals. Undoubtedly there were many more, as I am under the impression that a large number of the poems Dreiser contributed to magazines, the complete files of which I can not find, were used in parts in MOODS. But of course there is no way of telling this.

<table>
<tr><td>"The Poet"</td><td>New York Evening Post Literary Review; Dec. 20, 1924</td></tr>
<tr><td>"Tall Towers"</td><td>N. Y. Eve. Post. Lit. Review; Dec. 20, 1924</td></tr>
<tr><td>"Proteus"</td><td>The American Mercury; January 1924</td></tr>
<tr><td>"Wood Note"</td><td>Smart Set; May 1916</td></tr>
<tr><td>"The Stream"</td><td>Vanity Fair; April 1926</td></tr>
<tr><td>"Geddo Street"</td><td>Vanity Fair; April 1926</td></tr>
<tr><td>"For A Moment The Wind Died"</td><td>Smart Set; May 1916
The American Mercury; January 1924</td></tr>
<tr><td>"The Victim Speaks"</td><td>Vanity Fair; February 1927</td></tr>
<tr><td>"In A Country Graveyard"</td><td>N. Y. Eve. Post. Lit. Review; Dec. 20, 1924</td></tr>
<tr><td>"The Hidden God"</td><td>N. Y. Eve. Post. Lit. Review; Dec. 20, 1924</td></tr>
<tr><td>"The Little Flowers of Love and Wonder"</td><td>The American Mercury; January 1924</td></tr>
<tr><td>"Take Hands"</td><td>The American Mercury; January 1924</td></tr>
<tr><td>"The 'Bad' House"</td><td>Vanity Fair; April 1926</td></tr>
<tr><td>"The New Day"</td><td>New York Evening Post Literary Review; Dec. 20, 1924</td></tr>
<tr><td>"The Factory"</td><td>Vanity Fair; April 1926</td></tr>
<tr><td>"Ye Ages, Ye Tribes"</td><td>Smart Set; May 1916</td></tr>
<tr><td>"They Shall Fall as Stripped Garments"</td><td>Smart Set; May 1916</td></tr>
<tr><td>"The Great Blossom"</td><td>LEONARDO, New York, 1924-1925</td></tr>
</table>

The above poems that appeared in *The N. Y. Evening Post Literary Review* also appeared the next day in *The Philadelphia Public Ledger.*

[39] THE FINANCIER
(revised edition) *New York, 1927*

For years everybody had known, and many had expressed in print the obvious fact that THE FINANCIER was too long. For 15 years Dreiser had been thinking of re-writing it. Arrangements were made to have it revised and early in 1927 an almost new book emerged. The result is gratifying. It is 277 pages shorter than the original version, but the operation upon it consisted by no means of simply cutting out a paragraph here and there. In October,

1927, Constable of London published the English edition of this
new form. It will unquestionably be the book sold for THE FINAN-
CIER from now on, and wisely so.

[40] THE HAND OF THE POTTER
(revised edition) *New York, 1927*

On November 17, 1927, this book was published in a revised edition by Boni and Liveright. The revisions were made by Dreiser
in the last few pages of the last act of the play. It is a rather difficult volume to come by since no one was aware of revisions and
no copies were obtained by collectors.

[41] EINE AMERIKANISCHE TRAGODIE
Berlin (etc.) 1927

The first German translation by Marianne Schon was published
by P. Zsolnay in 3 volumes of 336, 376, and 416 pages.

[42] POORHOUSE SWEENEY
By Ed. Sweeney *New York, 1927*

Listed by McDonald, page 79.

[43] THE LANDGATE EDITION OF H. G. WELLS
New York, 1927

Only the first volume of this four volume edition brought out
by Duffield and Company, New York, contained the introduction
by Dreiser. This first volume was TONO BUNGAY.

[44] THOMAS HARDY: NOTES ON HIS LIFE AND WORK
n. d.

This 32 page booklet bound in red wrappers with a portrait of
Hardy and the title on front wrapper, was issued by Harpers for
advertising purposes. On page 15 was printed over Dreiser's name,
Dreiser's opinion of Hardy, which could have hardly been higher.
"*I rank him,*" says Dreiser here, "*with but one other, really . . .
Feodor Dostoievsky. ***In many respects, unless we return to Eurip-*

*ides and Sophocles, he is quite alone . . . a great Greek wandering
in a modern and hence an alien world.*" The pamphlet bears no date
but was issued not much before Hardy's death . . . probably in
1927.

[45] CHAINS
New York, 1927

The first trade edition (the limited was published later) was for
10,000 copies. Most of the stories in the book appeared in periodicals
and are listed as follows:

"Sanctuary"	*Smart Set*; October 1919
"The Hand"	*Munsey's*; May 1919
"Chains"	*Live Stories*; December 1920
"St. Colomba and The River"	*Pictorial Review*; January 1925. As Glory Be! McGlathery.
"Convention"	*The American Mercury*; December 1925
"The Old Neighborhood"	*Metropolitan Magazine*; December 1918
"Phantom Gold"	*Live Stories*; February 1921
"Marriage for One"	Syndicated in several newspapers October 1922. See McDonald, page 94 and 95. Also in MARRIAGE, New York 1923, a book by various authors.
"Fulfilment"	*Holland's Magazine*; February 1924
"The 'Mercy' Of God"	*The American Mercury*; August 1924

[46] THE SONGS OF PAUL DRESSER
New York, 1927

This book was brought out by Boni and Liveright in 1927 in an
edition of 2400 copies. It not only contains an introduction by
Dreiser but also the song *"On The Banks Of The Wabash,"* for
which Dreiser wrote the words. The introduction consisted in part
of *My Brother Paul*, a chapter in TWELVE MEN. It is, of course, a
legitimate, withal an amusing, Dreiser item. The reproductions of
the "1890" period lantern slides are worth the price of the book
alone. In connection with the book, the publishers printed on one
sheet of brown paper a broadside 7 3/4 by 5 inches headed
"Three Noted Song Writers & Publishers / On Paul Dresser's

Songs." It was issued in the book and should go with it to complete the item.

[47] THE ROAD TO BUENOS AYRES

By Albert Londres. *London, 1928*

This book, printed in London, carried an introduction by Dreiser. An edition brought out in the United States did not have the Dreiser contribution.

[48] THE CRIME OF DR. GARINE

By Boris Sokoloff. *New York, 1928*

This volume, published in New York by Covici-Friede, had an introduction by Dreiser.

[49] DREISER LOOKS AT RUSSIA

New York, 1928

This book is the result of a trip Dreiser made to Russia at the invitation of the Soviet Government. Its collation follows:

TITLE PAGE

Theodore Dreiser / (a rule) / DREISER LOOKS / AT RUSSIA / (Publisher's device) / New York / (a rule) / Horace Liveright. 1928 / About the whole is a box made up of a double one point rule inside a bold wave rule. The type is printed in black, the box in red.

PAGES

Pp. viii plus 264. Consisting of (i) Half-Title; Dreiser Looks at Russia (verso); blank. (iii); title page, as above. (verso); copyright, 1928, by / Theodore Dreiser / Printed in the United States of America (v);' Contents / (verso); blank. (vi); Half-title; Dreiser Looks at Russia (verso); blank. Pp. 9-264 text. Head piece in black and white at beginning of each chapter.

BINDING

8 1/4 by 5 1/2 inches. Issued in black cloth, stamped in gold, red and blind. Front cover; Dreiser / looks at / Russia / (Russian scene stamped in gold on red background, whole enclosed in box of one point rule, the rule stamped in gold). / Theodore Dreiser (Backbone) Dreiser / looks at / Russia / Theodore / Dreiser / (publisher's device) / Horace / Liveright

(the type stamped in gold, the device blind stamped). Back cover blank.
Top edge trimmed, others uncut. All edges white. Lining papers white.

DUST JACKET

White paper, front cover title and author's name in black ink. An illustration in three colors. Backbone ditto. Back cover has blurb of Dreiser's
A BOOK ABOUT MYSELF with portrait of Dreiser. Inside flaps have
blurb on Dreiser Looks at Russia. The title, on the front flap, is printed
in red ink.

[50] THEODORE DREISER, A BIBLIOGRAPHY
By Edward D. McDonald *Philadelphia, 1928*

The title of this book reads: A Bibliography / of the Writings
of / Theodore Dreiser. There was also a limited edition consisting
of 35 numbered copies signed by McDonald, 25 of which were for
sale. The trade edition was of 300 numbered copies.

[51] DER TITAN: TRILOGIE DER BEGIERDE
Berlin (etc.), 1928

This first German edition was translated by M. Schon and W.
Cremer and published by P. Zsolnay in three volumes of 527, 475
and 483 pages, respectively.

[52] MOODS, CADENCED AND DECLAIMED
[revised edition] *New York, 1928*

The trade edition, published by Boni and Liveright in September,
1928, is illustrated by Hugh Gray Lieber with 15 drawings entitled
"Symbols" which makes this issue the first illustrated edition. But
more important, there were changes in this issue. Twenty-nine
poems were added that did not appear in the signed limited edition
of 1926. The latter ended on page 328 and the trade edition ends
on page 385, indicating the inclusion of 57 pages of new material,
quite an important factor. It may be called the first revised edition.

TITLE PAGE

Moods / Cadenced & / Declaimed / By / Theodore / Dreiser / (type ornament) / With Fifteen Symbols by / Hugh Gray Lieber / (type ornament)
/ New York / Boni & Liveright / 1928 (the whole surrounded by an

58

ornamental border ⅝ inches wide printed in brown ink. The lettering is
in black ink. The type ornaments in brown). (Verso); Copyright, 1926,
1928, by / Theodore Dreiser / Printed in the United States of America

[53] NOTES TO ADD TO A BIBLIOGRAPHY OF THEODORE DREISER

By Vrest Orton   *[New York,] 1928*

This pamphlet is touched upon in the introduction to this book.
It measured 10 1/4 by 7 inches and consisted of 24 pages.

[54] THE ARGONAUT MANUSCRIPT EDITION OF THE WRITINGS OF FRANK NORRIS

Garden City, 1928

Contains an introduction by Dreiser. This edition, published in
December, 1928, was limited to 245 numbered sets of 10 volumes
each. The volume MCTEAGUE contained the introduction by
Dreiser. In 1929 the trade edition of these books was brought out.

[55] TWELVE MEN

New York, [1929]

The first Modern Library edition, which has an introduction by
Robert Ballou. Note: Copyright page carries caption "*First Modern
Library Edition, 1928.*"
This volume has a most attractive format.

[56] CATALOGUE OF AN EXHIBITION OF PAINTINGS

By Jerome Blum   *New York, 1929*

This four page folder was issued by The Anderson Galleries to
list on the back page the paintings of Mr. Blum. It is devoted to
an appreciation of Blum's works by Dreiser.

[57] THE ART-SENSATION OF NEW YORK!

[New York, 1929]

A four page folder on grey paper announcing the opening of the
Film Guild Cinema in New York, February 2nd, 1929. Part of the
2nd page has a foreword by Dreiser entitled, "Dreiser on Hollywood."

[58] THE ASPIRANT
    (Poetry Quartos) *New York, 1929*

This single poem was printed for the first time in *The Poetry Quartos*, a series of 12 four page pamphlets printed, illustrated and designed by Mr. Paul Johnston and published by Random House, New York. Each of the 12 contained a poem by a different author. The one containing THE ASPIRANT was bound in tan wrappers with an illustration on the front cover. The title page read:

THE ASPIRANT / (a star) / By Theodore Dreiser / (Publisher's device) / Random House, New York / 1929
Whole enclosed with two single rules and line of stars all around outside. Page 5, text.

[59] THE CARNEGIE WORKS AT PITTSBURGH
Chelsea, New York (n.d.)

Privately printed. One of 27 copies on Marlowe Antique Paper, Large 800, red buckram, as in the "1900 Sister Carrie", bevelled board, uncut. Illustrations on title in grey, orange rule at bottom, headband and initial letter in color. Laid in a page of the original Mss. on yellow manilla. Apparently a "stray" Dreiser item, printed for private distribution. As far as we can discover this is the first and only appearance of the essay in any form. It is possible that this was prepared for use in the series Dreiser wrote for "Success" Magazine. The book is of unusual interest to the collection. We know of no other Dreiser volume to contain a Mss.

[60] A GALLERY OF WOMEN
New York, 1929

This new Dreiser book, announced now for over a year, is finally scheduled for definite publication in November, 1929. Horace Liveright, Inc. the publishers, state regarding this book: "*In order to settle some questions which have been put to us by Dreiser's followers who have been reading his book* THIS MADNESS, *in Cosmopolitan Magazine, we beg to announce that* A GALLERY OF WOMEN *is an entirely separate and distinct work of fiction.*" Yet in *The Cosmopolitan*, the stories Rella, Olive Brand, and Regina C— appeared before the serial entitled "This Madness" was begun.

The trade edition, in two volumes, will undoubtedly consist of a large number of copies. In addition, there will be a limited edition of 560 copies of which 535 will be for sale. These numbered copies are to be autographed by Dreiser.

[61] MY CITY
New York, 1929

Another book scheduled for November, 1929, by Liveright is this work, consisting, according to the publishers, of a poem. It will be printed in a limited edition of about 500 numbered copies. Each copy will be signed. Illustrations are to be by Max Polleck, and will be in the form of colored etchings . . . eight in number. No trade edition is planned at the present.

[62] EPITAPH
New York, 1929

This is still another new volume to be published by the Heron Press this autumn but not early enough to be described in this book. The publishers give the following pre-view:

> "EPITAPH is Dreiser at his best. Sombre as the notes of a cello, beautiful and clear as the setting sun in all its glory, moving and spiritually exciting, it carries the reader into an abyss of emotional despair . . . 'I will never never pray again!' . . . and beyond that to a stark and clear, a daring and icily proud spiritualism. You might call it blasphemous . . . some will, no doubt, you might term it sinister . . . it is. But nobody will be able to escape its rhythm and its majesty."

That blurb about Dreiser's last book to be included here, is indeed worthy of preservation. No better example could be given to indicate how far the American estimation of Dreiser has come since the first days of SISTER CARRIE, thirty years ago.

The edition will consist of 1100 numbered copies, divided as follows: 1-100 on handmade Van Gelder, bound in flexible hand-tooled leather; signed by author and illustrator, 101-250 on hand-made Keijyo Kami, bound in Japanese silk, signed, 250-1100 on Keijyo Kami, bound in balloon cloth.

PART II

DREISER'S CONTRIBUTIONS TO PERIODICALS

Prof. McDonald is certainly correct when he says in his book that no one could pretend to have assembled in a limited time a complete list of the articles, poems and stories that Dreiser contributed to periodicals. I doubt if any one, even with *unlimited* time at one's disposal, could compile a definitive and complete list of such things. In the first place Dreiser himself seems to remember very little about the early pieces he sold to magazines. This can be seen by examining the preface to THE COLOR OF A GREAT CITY where, for the first time, Dreiser gives some clue to the first appearance of his written work. He does not, however, come near enough to be of any great help to the bibliographer who would run to earth these elusive magazine pieces. Dreiser, in that preface, mentions at least six of the chapters in the book as previously having appeared in magazines but no such magazines or appearances can be found by McDonald. I recall that Dreiser said he never kept any record of his earlier contributions. It must be seen that no assistance can be expected then from that quarter. It is *chance* as McDonald says that brings these things to light.

In the second place, the magazines to which we know, and others to which we believe Dreiser contributed do not exist anywhere (with one or two exceptions) in complete files. I have in mind especially those that come before 1900. The periodicals *The Voice*, *The Broadway Magazine*, *Era*, *Truth*, *Demorest's* and *Success* have been examined by me but only in parts in the New York Public Library. *The Puritan*, *The Voice*, *The Broadway Magazine*, *The Booklover*, *Every Month*, *Piano Music*, and *Demorests* have been scanned with a fine tooth comb by the Library of Congress. *Reedy's Mirror* is another early and most interesting magazine that can not be found in a complete file. Parts have been examined by Miss Isabel Devoy of The St. Louis Mercantile Library. Of the above named magazines in which no signed Dreiser material can be discovered may be mentioned *The Voice* and *The Booklover*. It is too bad that some of these early American magazines have not been preserved.

Somewhere, Dreiser has said that in 1899 he contributed to *The Voice* an article on John Burroughs. He also speaks of having articles in *The Ledger Monthly*, about which nothing is known. At another time Dreiser mentions a trolley trip to Boston that he made and wrote an article about. He speaks at some length about *Theodore Timby*, the true inventor of the revolving turret, who was cheated out of his invention by Ericson. He wrote an article about this and published it but he does not know where.

The difficulty must, therefore, be seen in getting together any great number of contributions to periodicals in addition to those listed by McDonald and those in this book. McDonald finds and sets down, to take one period for instance, some 35 articles and poems in magazines before 1900. In my list of addenda that follows here will be found about 54 more of the same period. McDonald says that Dreiser, when he examined McDonald's list of some 150 contributions to periodicals, was indeed surprised that he had ever written so many. To this entire list I add some 110 more, making a grand total of well over 250 appearances of Dreiser writings in periodicals during 30 years. It would seem that the greater proportion of such things are now listed.

Dreiser's first published piece of writing appeared in October, 1891, being a description of Chicago's worst slum. Dreiser wrote this piece for the *Chicago Globe* and also contributed other pieces to its Sunday Section. Four years later he was in New York where he edited a little magazine called *Every Month* for the Hawley Haviland Company, the publisher of his brother Paul Dresser's music. His work on this sheet began in October, 1895, and continued until April, 1897, and it consisted of all of the editorials and most of the long reviews.

For the handy guidance of those who may wish to examine and collect Dreiser's stuff as it appeared in newspapers from 1891 to 1895 when he began to write in magazines, I list the following, culled from A BOOK ABOUT MYSELF.

1 Articles and poems in *Chicago Globe*, mostly in Sunday Section, from January, 1891 to November, 1892. The poems were printed under the name of Carl Dreiser. The last work on *The Globe* consisted of series of articles about fake auction shops.

2 *St. Louis Globe Democrat*. Dreiser's first article in this paper apart from regular news reporting, was a double page spread in The Sunday Supplement about the new depot. Here he later conducted a daily column called "Heard in The Corridors," which was about hotel arrivals in St. Louis. It was often fiction. Many of his articles were interviews with celebrities who came to town. His first real front page scoop was a piece, illustrated with drawings, about the great train wreck in Alton. He also conducted the dramatic column.

3 *The St. Louis Republic.* His first feature work here was a series of comic stories about baseball. This was followed by a series to boost a popularity contest amongst school teachers, the winners later attending the World's Fair in Chicago, with Dreiser as guide and mentor. In 1893 he did many other specials for the Sunday Section.

4 In 1893 he went to Toledo where he wrote a piece about the street car strike which piece appeared in the *Toledo Bee*.

5 In Cleveland in *The Cleveland Leader* his first story was a write-up of a chicken ranch for the Sunday Supplement.

6 Pittsburgh. Here he did stuff for the *Dispatch* from April 1894. The first piece was an allegory about a fly.

7 In New York he wrote a little for *The World*. His first piece was a story of an East Side brawl.

In the last half of 1929 Dreiser has been writing a good deal for newspapers and magazines in Europe.

In the last two years Dreiser contributed two series of articles to American syndicates which appeared in a long list of American newspapers who used this service. Since these pieces were printed not as news but as articles, they may in reality be considered amongst contributions to periodicals.

Beginning April 10, 1927, Dreiser wrote a series of articles for The Metropolitan Syndicate which was at the time running a feature series under the general head of LOVE, WOMEN AND MARRIAGE. Many well known writers contributed articles to this series. The articles that Dreiser wrote were widely sold to newspapers throughout the country, and especially to the Hearst group. They appeared illustrated in the section of the Hearst papers entitled MARCH OF EVENTS on Sundays only.

The titles of Dreiser's articles were:

1—Is America's Restlessness A Symbol of Her Hidden Power? April 10, 1927.
2—Are We in America Leading The Way to a Golden Age in The World? May 22, 1927.
3—Fools of Success. July 31, 1927.
4—Fools of Love. August 28, 1927.
5—Dreiser Analyzes Rebellion of Women. February 5, 1928.
6—On Matrimonial Hoboes. March 11, 1928.

In 1928 beginning March 18th, Dreiser did a series of eleven articles for the *North American Newspaper Alliance*. These articles appeared in several newspapers notably the *New York World* and were later incorporated into Dreiser Looks At Russia.

1—Soviet Plans to Spread to United States. March 18, 1928.
2—Dreiser Looks at Russia. (General heading) March 19, 1928 (Sub-title) Earnest efforts made to provide pleasant working conditions and some laborers get more than Stalin.
3—Not converted to communism but greatly impressed with efforts to apply theories of Marx. March 20, 1928
4—Many hardships are suffered by the working class, but all seem anxious to better conditions. March 21, 1928
5—Dreadful sense of social misery removed under Soviet system . . . few suggestions of differences between classes. March 22, 1928
6—Net work of propaganda spread over Russia . . . posters and pamphlets in all public places. March 23, 1928
7—Soviet determination to re-educate all citizens robs nation of able play production. March 24, 1928
8—Government directed by Communist party, employs labor like capitalist trust, demanding absolute loyalty. March 25, 1928
9—Propaganda fills schools and red flags adorn nurseries to inculcate spirit of communism. March 26, 1928
10—Atmosphere of military preparation pervades nation, army active and well distributed. March 27, 1928
11—Strenuous efforts made to shackle greed . . . many grafters shot or sent to prison. March 28, 1928

CONTRIBUTIONS TO PERIODICALS
By Theodore Dreiser
(Not listed by McDonald)

Our Women Violinists	*The Puritan,* Nov. 1897
On The Field of the Brandywine	*Truth Magazine,* Nov. 6, 1897
Craze For A New Disease	*Every Month,* 1897
Henry Mosler, A Painter For the People (Illus)	*Demorest's Family Magazine,* February, 1898
A Photographic Talk with Edison (Illus)	*Success,* February 1898
Virtue (A Poem)	*Demorest's,* Sept. 1898
Anthony Hope Tells a Secret (Illus)	*Success,* March, 1898
Resignation (Poem)	*Demorest's,* April 1898
How William Dean Howells Climbed Fame's Ladder. (Illus)	*Success,* April 1898
Artists' Studios. Hints Concerning The Aim of All Decoration (Illus)	*Demorest's,* June 1898
With Whom Is Shadow Turning (Poem)	*Demorest's,* June 1898
Carrier Pigeons in War Time, Their Use On Warships And Capabilities in Carrying Swift Information (Illus)	*Demorest's,* July 1898

If Force Transmutes (Poem) .... *Demorest's, Aug. 1899*
A Notable Colony. Artistic and Literary People in the Picturesque Bronx—Who They Are and How They Live. (Illus) .... *Demorest's, Aug. 1899*
It Pays To Treat Workers Generously. (Illus) This was written about John H. Patterson, the cash register magnate. .... *Success, Sept. 16, 1899*
American Women Violinists. (Illus) .... *Success, Sept. 30, 1899*
C. C. Curran (Illus) .... *Truth, Sept. 1899*
Curious Shift of the Poor (Illus) .... *Demorest's, Nov. 1899*
American Women Who Are Winning Fame As Pianists, (Illus) .... *Success, Nov. 4, 1899*
The Unrewarded (Poem) .... *Demorest's, Nov. 1899*
Our Government And Our Food (Illus) .... *Demorest's, Dec. 1899*
John Burroughs .... *The Voice, 1899*
Little Clubman of the Tenements .... *Puritan, Feb. 1900*
New York's Underground Railroad (Illus) .... *Pearson's, April 1900*
Good Roads for Bad. (Illus) .... *Pearson's, May 1900*
The Railroads and the People. (Reprint in part from this article as it appeared in Harper's Monthly, for February 1900) ...... *Review of Reviews, March 1900*
The History of the Horse .... *Everybody's, June 1900*
The Transmigration of the Sweat Shop............ *The Puritan, July 1900*
When the Old Century was New: A Love Story (Illus) .... *Pearson's, January 1901*
The Rural Free Mail Delivery (Illus)............ *Pearson's, Feb. 1901*
Lawrence E. Earl (Illus) .... *Truth, Feb. 1901*
Plant Life Underground (Illus) .... *Pearson's, June 1901*
Butcher Rogaum's Door .... *Reedy's Mirror, Dec. 12, 1901*
A Cripple Whose Energy Gives Inspiration. (Illus) An early short story, though the title would never reveal it. .... *Success, Feb. 1902*
A Touch of Human Brotherhood, (Illus) Another early short story...................... *Success, March, 1902*
The Tenement Toilers *** (Illus) .... *Success, April, 1902*
The Realization of an Ideal.................... *Tom Watson's Magazine, 1905*
The Flight of Pigeons (Illus)................... *The Bohemian Magazine, October 1909*
Paris (Illus) .... *The Century Magazine, Oct. 1913*
Why Attack Books (Portrait) .... *Independent, March 1917*
The Right to Kill .... *The Call, 1919*
Hollywood Now .... *McCall's Magazine, Sept. 1921*
Why Not Tell Europe about Bertha M. Clay (Reprinted from St. Paul Daily News)........ *The N. Y. Call, Oct. 21, 1921*
Hollywood, Its Morals and Manners (General Heading)
  1—The Struggle on the Threshold of Moving Pictures .... *Shadowland, Nov. 1921*
  2—The Commonplace Tale with a Thousand Endings .... *Shadowland, Dec. 1921*
  3—The Beginner's Thousand to One Chance *Shadowland, Jan. 1922*
  4—The Extra's Fight to Exist.................... *Shadowland, Feb. 1922*
Applied Religion—Applied Art .... *The Survey, May 1, 1923*

Author's League of America (Letter) .... *Century*, Sept. 1923
The Irish Section Foreman Who Taught Me How To Live .... *Hearst's Magazine*, Aug. 1924
The Most Successful Ball-Player of Them All. (Illus) (An Interview with Ty Cobb). ...... *Hearst's Magazine*, Feb. 1925
Chauncey M. Depew .... *Hearst's*, July, 1925
Interview. (Front page signed interview with man condemned to death for murder)........ *N. Y. Morning World*, Nov. 1925
Marriage, This Is What I Think About It. (Illus) An Interview with Dreiser but containing direct quotation by him. .... *Success*, Nov. 1925.
Marriage For One .... *Crescenta Valley Ledger*, March 1926
Music (Poem) .... *Vanity Fair*, June 1926
Recent Poems of Love and Sorrow .... *Vanity Fair*, Sept. 1926
Recent Poems of Youth and Age........................ *Vanity Fair*, Oct. 1926
Wages of Sin .... *Cosmopolitan*, Oct. 1926
America's Restlessness Is a Symbol of Our Hidden Power. (A serial syndicated feature which ran from April 10, 1927 to March 11, 1928) .... *N. Y. American* and other Hearst Papers
Can a Criminal Come Back to Society? "No". *Smoker's Companion Magazine*, May 1927
Rella .... *Cosmopolitan*, April 1928
Russian Vignettes (Illus) .... *The Saturday Evening Post*, April 28, 1928
Olive Brand .... *Cosmopolitan*, May 1928
Russia, The Great Experiment .... *Vanity Fair*, June 1928
Regina C— .... *Cosmopolitan*, June 1928
Best Motion Picture Interview Ever Written *Photoplay*, August 1928
Citizens of Moscow (Illus) .... *Vanity Fair*, Oct. 1928
My City (This poem was translated into a dozen languages and published all over the world) .... *N. Y. Herald-Tribune* Dec. 23, 1928
How Russia Handles the Sex Question (Port) *Current History*, January 1929
Muffled Oar (A poem) .... *The Nation*, Feb. 27, 1929
Another American Tragedy: Reply to G. K. Chesterton .... *Forum*, March 1929
Portrait of An Artist .... *Vanity Fair*, April 1929
The Meddlesome Decade; How Censorship is Making our Civilization Ridiculous .... *Theatre Guild Magazine*, May, 1929
This Madness—An Honest Novel about Love. *Hearst's International (Cosmopolitan)* Illus. A serial which ran from Feb. 1929 through every month to and including July, 1929. Six installments, each story complete in 2 issues.

PART III

DREISER MANUSCRIPTS

In 1922 Mr. W. W. Lange determined to assemble a set of the original manuscripts of Dreiser's books. To aid this effort, Dreiser described the Mss. that were in his possession as well as those which were already sold. It is of considerable interest to the collector, I believe, to have this evidence in print.

The Ms. of SISTER CARRIE on yellow copy paper was presented to Henry L. Mencken years before. Mencken would not part with it for love or money and it is in his possession today. The first version in pen of JENNIE GERHARDT Mr. Lange purchased from Dreiser who bought it back some years afterward. THE FINANCIER original Ms. was in handwriting and consisted of 80 chapters, although the book had only 74. In some strange fashion this Ms. became lost. THE TITAN in the original pen version had over 80 chapters but in the published form had only 61. The final chapters were greatly changed at the last hour, in proof. Dreiser had this Ms. in his possession in 1922. He also owned the pen version of THE "GENIUS" which covered 104 chapters, the book when published having only 102. A TRAVELER AT FORTY, in pen copy, was destroyed but was originally a good deal longer than the published edition. The Mss. of the plays going to make up PLAYS OF THE NATURAL AND THE SUPERNATURAL were split up and some sold. A HOOSIER HOLIDAY was written in pen on small pages, and it had much material that did not appear in the book. Dreiser possessed this. FREE, existing in pen versions was also split up and some Mss. sold. THE HAND OF THE POTTER was partially typed and partially written with a pen. The last scene was re-written for the book. The Ms. belonged to Dreiser. Dreiser also had the 12 Mss. going to make up TWELVE MEN. HEY RUB-A-DUB-DUB Mss. were destroyed. A BOOK ABOUT MYSELF, in pen, was much longer than the printed form. At this time (1922) Alfred Goldsmith owned the Ms. of THE BLUE SPHERE, David Karsner had LAUGHING GAS and William E. Lengel THE GIRL IN THE COFFIN. James A. Ettinge owned THE LOST PHOEBE and George T. Keating FREE.

It is well known that Dreiser is in the habit of making multitudinous corrections and addenda on the galley proofs of his books. Sometimes, indeed, he nearly writes a book over on the proof sheets. For this reason, it is not probable that many original Mss. of his books are at all like the published versions.

75

PART IV

REVIEWS AND STUDIES ABOUT DREISER IN BOOKS AND PAMPHLETS

A list of this sort can not possibly be complete. Dozens of books have been written during the last thirty years about American Literature which might have mentioned Dreiser. The most important ones are doubtless listed either in McDonald's list of (30) such volumes or in mine of (54) which follows. There are countless school books on the subject used as texts in secondary schools which there has been no attempt to discover. They can be of little importance. The following either mention Dreiser or devote whole chapters to him and his books. During the last 15 years, at least, there must also have been a good many pamphlets, folders, brochures and broadsides issued by the several publishers who had Dreiser's books at one time or another. These things are quickly lost and seldom saved. A few, however, of the most important, are listed here.

IN PAMPHLETS

1—THE HAND OF THE POTTER. A 10 page stapled booklet, 8 3/4 by 5 3/4. Undated, without pagination. Issued by Boni and Liveright in 1918 for advertising purposes. Contains reviews, letters and excerpts.

2—FREE AND OTHER STORIES. An eight page stapled booklet, 8 1/2 by 6. Issued in 1920 by Boni and Liveright for advertising purposes. Contains reprints of reviews. Not dated.

3—A BOOK ABOUT THEODORE DREISER AND HIS WORK. This 24 page stapled booklet, 6 x 3 1/4 inches, was issued by Boni and Liveright in 1926 for advertising purposes. It was printed on brown antique laid paper and bound in darker brown stiff wrappers. The front cover had *Theodore Dreiser* printed in red in center, and above and below it, a list of Dreiser's books, with publisher's name *Boni and Liveright* at bottom. Frontispiece was a drawing of Dreiser by Hydeman in black and white, printed on white paper and pasted in. It had a facsimile signature at bottom. This booklet was partially a reprint of the one issued by Lane in 1916-1917 (See McDonald page 105). It contained a new appreciation by Sherwood Anderson (One of the best things of its kind ever written) and a piece *The Case of Dreiser* by H. L. Mencken, another remarkably interesting critical valuation. Between these two pieces was *Theodore Dreiser; a Portrait* by Edgar Lee Masters, a poem which appeared in the Lane pamphlet. Following were reviews of 15 of Dreiser's books, with one page *Biographical Note* at end. This and the Lane pamphlet are two most valuable things of this kind. The Lane pamphlet was reissued in same size, without brown wrappers, printed on yellow paper with cover in black ink instead of gold. The contents were the same. . . . The one first being issued being more elaborate, with its extra cover.

IN BOOKS

A DICTIONARY OF AMERICAN AUTHORS. *Edited* by Oscar Adams. Boston, 1901.
This book, probably the first to print a biographical note of Dreiser,

79

refers in a small note to STUDIES OF CONTEMPORARY CELEBRITIES and to
POEMS as being published volumes by Dreiser. Of Dreiser it says he is
"a litterateur in New York City."

THE SPIRIT OF AMERICAN LITERATURE. By John Macy. New
York, (1913).
This is one of the first popular books on American Literature to include
Dreiser amongst worthwhile American writers. It refers twice to JENNIE
GERHARDT published the year before.

ONE HUNDRED BEST BOOKS. By John Cowper Powys, New York,
1916.
Refers to Dreiser.

THE FUN I GET OUT OF LIFE. By E. Haldeman-Julius. Girard,
Kansas.
On page 79 of this Blue Book No. B-8 there is a short essay cn Dreiser.

HORIZONS: A Book of Criticism. By Francis Hackett. New York, 1918.
Refers to Dreiser.

OUR AMERICA. By Waldo Frank. New York, 1919.
The chapter headed "Chicago" contains material about Dreiser. The
English edition of this book was entitled NEW AMERICA.

AMERICAN WRITERS OF THE PRESENT DAY. By T. E. Rankin.
Ann Arbor, 1920.
In which a professor of Rhetoric classes Dreiser with Mr. Owen Johnson
and declares that Dreiser violates convention "uncreatively" and that he
"should go to school to George Eliot."

THE GOLDEN DAY. By Lewis Mumford. New York, 1921.
Contains a fine estimation of Dreiser as a literary artist.

LETTERS ON CONTEMPORARY AMERICAN AUTHORS. By Martin
MacCollough. Boston, 1921.
One of these chapters is about Dreiser.

THE CAMBRIDGE HISTORY OF AMERICAN LITERATURE. New
York, 1921.
In this great history of American Literature and authors Dreiser gets no
mention except a passing one by Mr. Montrose Moses who speaks of
Dreiser as author of a one-act play. The position of Dreiser as a novelist
had apparently not been called to the editor's attention.

THE NOVEL OF TOMORROW. By Twelve American Novelists. In-
dianapolis, (1922).
Mr. William Allen White mentions Dreiser. Dreiser was to have contributed his essay to this volume which first appeared in the *New Republic*, April 12, 1922 but made other arrangements at the last moment.

AMERICAN LITERATURE. By Thomas E. Rankin. New York, (1922).
Mentions Dreiser.

APPRAISEMENTS AND ASPERITIES AS TO SOME CONTEMPO-
RARY WRITERS. By Felix Schelling. Philadelphia, 1922.

Refers to CAIUS GRACCHUS and Dreiser's foreword to it.

ESSAYS AND MISCELLANIES. By Joseph S. Auerbach. New York, 1922.

Refers to the suppression of THE "GENIUS." Mr. Auerbach was the lawyer who handled the case.

THE CYCLOPAEDIA OF AMERICAN BIOGRAPHY. *Edited* by J. F.
Homans and H. M. Linen. N. Y., 1922.

There is, in this compilation, a surprisingly long sketch of Dreiser inaccurately written by some unknown hand. It speaks of Dreiser's first book as having been published by Appleton in 1900. It quotes from a review which had appeared in the *London Academy* which review had said that SISTER CARRIE was the best work of fiction ever to be published in America.

THE LITERARY RENAISSANCE IN AMERICA. By C. E. Bechhofer.
[Carl Eric Bechhofer Roberts.] London, [1923].

Mentions Dreiser several times.

BACKGROUNDS OF BOOK REVIEWING. *Edited* by S. S. Mallory.
(Ann Arbor, Michigan) 1923.

Contains "The Barbaric Naturalism of Theodore Dreiser" by Stuart Sherman.

HORSES AND MEN. By Sherwood Anderson. New York, 1923.

This book is dedicated to Dreiser and has a prefatory paragraph about him.

THE DEVELOPMENT OF THE AMERICAN SHORT STORY. By Fred
Lewis Pattee. New York, 1923.

Refers to Dreiser.

THE ADVANCE OF THE AMERICAN SHORT STORY. By Edward
J. O'Brien. New York, 1923.

Refers to Dreiser, especially the story "The Lost Phoebe."

NEW INTERNATIONAL ENCYCLOPAEDIA. New York, 1923.

Volume 7 contains a biographical sketch of Dreiser. Although the volume is dated 1923, this piece must have been written sometime before 1914.

PEOPLE YOU KNOW. By "Young Boswell" (pseud., Harold Stark)
New York, 1924.

Contains an interview with Dreiser entitled, THE "GENIUS." It was originally published in *The New York Tribune*, April 7, 1923.

AMERICAN AND BRITISH LITERATURE SINCE 1880. By Carl and
Mark Van Doren. New York, 1925.

There is a chapter devoted to Dreiser.

THE ENCYCLOPAEDIA AMERICANA. New York, 1925.
Vol. 9 has a note on Dreiser.

MEYER'S LEXIKON. Leipzig, 1925.
Vol. 3 has a short note about Dreiser. This is apparently the first foreign encyclopaedia to mention Dreiser. The French, Spanish and Italian compilations have not yet taken notice of him.

THE VERDICT OF BRIDLEGOOSE. By Llewellyn Powys. New York, 1926.
Dreiser is referred to in the chapter headed "Friends."

THE OUTLOOK FOR AMERICAN PROSE. By Joseph Warren Beach. Chicago (1926).
Refers to Dreiser.

AMERIKANISCHE PROSA vom Burgerkrieg bis auf die Gegenwart (1863-1922). Von Dr. Walther Fischer. Leipzig, Berlin, 1926.
Refers to Dreiser.

ANTHOLOGIE de la LITTÉRATURE AMÉRICAINE. Par C. Cestre [et] B. Gagnot. Paris, 1926.
On pages 143 and 144 there is a biographical note on Dreiser. On pages 144 to 148 appears Chapter XXVI of THE "GENIUS" translated into French under the title "Visite á un Médecin de Science Chrétienne." This should also be listed under the heading of books containing contributions by Dreiser.

LE ROMAN AMÉRICAINE d' AUJOURD'HUI. Par Regis Michaud. Paris, (1926).
Later translated and published in America under title of THE AMERICAN NOVEL TODAY (see below).

EMERSON AND OTHERS. By Van Wyck Brooks. New York, (1927).
Refers to Dreiser in chapter "The Literary Life in America."

THE LITERARY REVOLUTION. By Stanton A. Coblentz. New York, 1927.
Refers to Dreiser.

A PRIMER OF BOOK COLLECTING. By John Tracy Winterich. New York, 1927.
Mr. Winterich, one of America's foremost writers on the subject of collecting books pays some attention here to Dreiser as a "collected author."

THE FIRST HUNDRED MILLION. By E. Haldeman-Julius, New York, 1928.
In which the sale of Dreiser's books is discussed.

COLLECTORS' CHOICE. By John Tracy Winterich. New York, (1928).
Several of Dreiser's first additions are mentioned.

SPOKESMEN: MODERN WRITERS AND AMERICAN LIFE. By T.
    K. Whipple. New York, 1928.
  There is a chapter on Dreiser.

DESTINATIONS: A CANVAS OF AMERICAN LITERATURE. SINCE
    1900. By Gorham B. Munson. New York [1928].
  Refers to Dreiser.

CONTEMPORARY AMERICAN AUTHORS. By J. C. Squire and
    associated critics of *The London Mercury*. *Introduction* by Henry
    Seidel Canby. New York, (1928).
  Contains "Theodore Dreiser" by Milton Waldman.

TO THE PURE: A Study in Obscenity and The Censor. By Morris Ernst.
    New York, 1928.
  Refers many times to Dreiser and his books which came to the attention
of the censors.

AMERICAN CRITICISM. By Norman Foerster. New York, 1928.
  Refers to Dreiser.

THE RE-INTERPRETATION OF AMERICAN LITERATURE. *Edited*
    by Norman Foerster. New York, 1928.
  Refers to Dreiser.

SIXTEEN AUTHORS TO ONE. By David Karsner. New York, 1928.
  Karsner knew Dreiser and here* writes about Dreiser biographically and
bibliographically.
*In one chapter.

THE AMERICAN NOVEL TODAY. By Regis Michaud. Boston, 1928.
  Two chapters of this book are devoted to Dreiser and his work.

NELSON'S PERPETUAL LOOSE-LEAF ENCYCLOPAEDIA. *Edited* by
    John H. Finley. New York [1928].
  Vol. 4 has a biographical note.

OUTLINE OF BUNK. By E. Haldeman-Julius. Boston, 1929.
  Mentions Dreiser several times.

THE BIG AMERICAN PARADE. By E. Haldeman-Julius. Boston, 1929.
  In Chapter XV Dreiser is discussed.

THE AMERICAN NOVEL. By Grant Overton. Philadelphia, 1929.
  In which this author with bizaare judgment concludes in surveying
Dreiser's work that "The Titan," "The Financier" and "Jennie Gerhardt"
are novels that "need not be read."

AMERICAN LITERATURE: An Interpretive Survey. By Ernest S. Leisy.
    New York (1929).
  Refers to Dreiser.

AMERICAN FIRST EDITIONS. *Edited* by Merle Johnson. New York,
    1929.
Amongst the some hundred and five authors included is a bibliographical
check-list of the first editions of Dreiser, compiled by W. W. Lange and
Vrest Orton. The list was not without errors.

CONTEMPORARY AMERICAN LITERATURE. (Revised edition). By
    John M. Manly. Chicago, 1929.
Mentions Dreiser.

THE ENCYCLOPAEDIA BRITANNICA (14th edition). New York,
    1929.
There is a biographical and critical article in this compilation written by
William Rose Benét. This marks Dreiser's first appearance in the Britannica.